NORTH VIETNAM'S 1972 EASTER OFFENSIVE

HANOI'S GAMBLE

STEPHEN EMERSON

Pen & Sword
MILITARY
AN IMPRINT OF PEN & SWORD BOOKS LTD.
YORKSHIRE – PHILADELPHIA

First published in Great Britain in 2020 by
PEN AND SWORD MILITARY
an imprint of
Pen and Sword Books Ltd
47 Church Street
Barnsley
South Yorkshire S70 2AS

ISBN 978 1 52675 712 8

A CIP record for this book is available from the British Library

Typeset by Aura Technology and Software Services, India
Maps and drawings by George Anderson
Printed and bound in England by TJ International Ltd., Padstow, Cornwall

Pen & Sword Books Ltd incorporates the imprints of Pen & Sword Archaeology, Atlas, Aviation, Battleground, Discovery, Family History, History, Maritime, Military, Naval, Politics, Railways, Select, Social History, Transport, True Crime, Claymore Press, Frontline Books, Leo Cooper, Praetorian Press, Remember When, Seaforth Publishing and Wharncliffe.

For a complete list of Pen and Sword titles please contact
Pen and Sword Books Limited
47 Church Street, Barnsley, South Yorkshire, S70 2AS, England
email: enquiries@pen-and-sword.co.uk
website: www.pen-and-sword.co.uk

or

Pen and Sword Books
1950 Lawrence Rd, Havertown, PA 19083, USA
email: uspen-and-sword@casematepublishers.com
www.penandswordbooks.com

FSC
www.fsc.org
MIX
Paper from responsible sources
FSC® C013056

CONTENTS

LIST OF MAPS AND GRAPHS

ACKNOWLEDGEMENTS

Special thanks to the National Museum of the Air Force in Dayton, Ohio and especially to archivist Brett Stolle for his invaluable assistance in helping me research the museum's data and photo collections.

I am grateful to the Department of the Air Force and the Department of the Navy, including the Air Force Historical Research Agency at Maxwell AFB, Alabama and the Naval History and Heritage Command in Washington, DC, for their commitment to enhancing public access to official photographic and documentary materials concerning the Vietnam War.

My deep appreciation to all those writers and researchers who have labored to document and analyze the 1972 Easter Offensive and thus provide greater understanding of this aspect of the Vietnam War. Especially invaluable were General Ngo Quong Truong Ngo's *The Easter Offensive of 1972* and his accompanying maps, Dale Andrade's *America's Last Vietnam Battle* (which fleshes out much of Truong's material), David Fulghum's and Terrance Maitland's *South Vietnam on Trial,* Thomas McKenna's *Kontum,* and Colonel Gerald Turley's *The Easter Offensive.* The work of Lien-Hang Nguyen, Merle Pribbenow, and Lam Quang Thi also provide an interesting view from the Vietnamese perspective that is well worth reading.

Finally, to the dozens of American military advisers, who stood shoulder to shoulder with their South Vietnamese counterparts on the front lines and faced down the North Vietnamese onslaught, their bravery and self-sacrifice inspired many of those around them at the most trying of times; theirs is an often forgotten story that should be remembered.

GLOSSARY

alpha strike	large-scale air strike against a fixed target
Arc Light	B-52 carpet bombing mission
ARVN	Army of the Republic of Vietnam (South Vietnam)
AT-3	Soviet-made wire-guided anti-tank weapon
Atoll missile	Soviet air-to-air missile used by MiG-21s that was a Soviet copy of the U.S. AIM-9 Sidewinder missile
chaff	thin strips of aluminum or coated fiberglass disbursed by aircraft to confuse enemy radar and weapons guidance systems
CORDS	Civilian Operations and Rural Development Support program
DMZ	demilitarized zone dividing North and South Vietnam
FAC	forward air controller
Iron Hand	SAM suppression mission
LAW	U.S.-made light anti-tank weapon; officially the M72
MACV	Military Assistance Command Vietnam
MR 1	Military Region 1, encompassing the 5 northern provinces of South Vietnam under I Corps area of responsibility.
MR 2	Military Region 2, encompassing the 13 provinces of central South Vietnam under II Corps area of responsibility.
MR 3	Military Region 3, encompassing the 11 provinces surrounding Saigon under III Corps area of responsibility.
MR 4	Military Region 4, encompassing the 15 provinces of the Mekong Delta under IV Corps area of responsibility.
NVA	North Vietnamese Army; officially known as the People's Army of Vietnam or PAVN
Operation Freedom Train	U.S. aerial interdiction campaign against North Vietnam, April 1972
Operation Linebacker	U.S. bombing campaign against North Vietnam, May–October 1972
Operation Rolling Thunder	U.S. bombing campaign against North Vietnam, 1965–1968
PF	Popular Forces; part of South Vietnamese territorial militia forces
POL	petroleum, oil, and lubricants

RF	Regional Forces; part of South Vietnamese territorial militia forces
SA-2	Soviet-made Guideline surface-to-air missile
SA-7	Soviet-made Strela handheld, portable surface-to-air missile
SAM	surface-to-air missile
TAW	tactical airlift wing (Air Force)
TFS	tactical fighter squadron (Air Force)
TFW	tactical fighter wing (Air Force)
TOW	U.S.-made tube-launched, optically tracked, wire-guided anti-tank weapon
TRW	tactical reconnaissance wing (Air Force)
VNAF	Republic of Vietnam Air Force (South Vietnam)
VPAF	Vietnamese People's Air Force (North Vietnam)
Wild Weasel	F-105G and F-4C air defense suppression and radar jamming aircraft (Air Force)
Yankee Station	Code name for Navy carrier operating point in the Gulf of Tonkin that supported air operations in North Vietnam, Laos, and South Vietnam

1. A GATHERING STORM

After nearly seven years of war the American military involvement in the Vietnam was coming to an end. The once-massive U.S. troop presence had fallen from a peak of nearly 550,000 to 156,000—less than a third of them combat troops—by January 1972 and was on track to fall below 70,000 by the spring as the burden of fighting the war shifted almost exclusively to Saigon's forces as the process of Vietnamization took hold. The Americans were clearly on their way out. It was now only a question of time and circumstance. Despite the lack of substantial progress at ongoing peace talks in Paris, President Richard Nixon and his national security adviser Henry Kissinger continued to pursue a two-track disengagement strategy of seeking a favorable negotiated peace settlement while also preparing the South Vietnamese to stand on their own in the aftermath of American disengagement. Either way as they saw it, Hanoi would be denied victory and there was little the North Vietnamese could do to change the situation. Or so Washington thought.

State of the Southern Battlefield

Although under no illusion that the war had reached a favorable turning point for the South Vietnamese government of President Nguyen Van Thieu by 1972, the strategic outlook for the United States on the surface appeared quite promising. Four years after the Tet Offensive, the Viet Cong insurgency had yet to recover to its pre-1968 levels, the Saigon government had steadily increased its control over the countryside and the population, and the South Vietnamese armed forces were well on their way to becoming the most modern and best equipped military in the region. Likewise, preemptive cross-border ground incursions into Cambodia and southern Laos in recent years, as well as an unrelenting American air interdiction campaign against the Ho Chi Minh Trail, had damaged and disrupted the North's logistics and infiltration network supporting the war in the South. Thus, at the very least, the Thieu government appeared well positioned to hold its own in the immediate aftermath of any American military disengagement.

Much of the reason for this optimism by General Creighton Abrams and his Military Assistance Command Vietnam (MACV) stemmed from the perceived successes of the Saigon government's accelerated pacification program to enhance rural security and strengthen the government's control over the population and in the prospects of Vietnamization yielding an effective counterweight—albeit with continuing U.S. security guarantees—to future North Vietnamese military aggression in the South.

By the early 1970s steady gains in the U.S.-assisted pacification effort, known as the Civilian Operations and Rural Development Support (CORDS) program, had allowed Saigon to extend its grip over vast reaches of the country, undermine the Viet Cong's political and military infrastructure, and shrink communist-controlled territory to isolated pockets and strategically insignificant areas along the sparely populated Cambodian and Laotian borders. Moreover, it was estimated that 95 percent of the South Vietnamese

Map 1: Southeast Asia Theater of Operations.

population now lived in "secure or relatively secure" areas, double the 1968 figure.[1] Under the mantra of "self-defense, self-government, and self-development," General Abrams made pacification "the number one strategy for the war."[2] The struggle now became one for the hearts and minds of the Vietnamese people at the village level and not one of locating and destroying enemy troops on the battlefield. Accordingly, greater emphasis was placed on growing the size and quality of self-defense forces to provide improved local security under the CORDS program. Not only had the size of these territorial militia forces grown to more than 550,000 by 1971, but they were now much better trained and equipped than in the past. And this in turn lifted much of the static defense burden from the Army of the Republic of Vietnam (ARVN), thus freeing up regular ARVN units for offensive operations. The results were so impressive that some observers believed that the southern Viet Cong-based insurgency "had been defeated."[3]

This pacification success, however, was not without controversy. The government's heavy reliance on harsh tactics and repressive measures, such as forced relocations, the use of free-fire zones, and the extra-judicial killings, often undermined government efforts to win over the rural population. Likewise, the building of grassroots democracy remained stillborn as almost without exception district officials were pulled from the ranks of the military and personally appointed by President Thieu for their loyalty rather than ability. Thus, Saigon's actions frequently created an atmosphere of fear and resentment against the regime and fealty to the government remained fleeting.

Hand in hand with strengthening the government's control over the countryside was the American drive to make Vietnamization a success and thus allow the Saigon regime to stand on its own two feet. While political necessity drove the Nixon administration to hand over responsibility for ground combat operations and ultimately the defense of the country to the South Vietnamese, the underlying military rationale also had merit. In helping to build

As commander U.S. Military Assistance Command, Vietnam (MACV), General Creighton Abrams was charged with overseeing the drawdown of American ground troops while still continuing to prosecute the war.

President Richard Nixon and his national security adviser Henry Kissinger sought to disengage from Vietnam while ensuring the viability of South Vietnam and maintaining U.S. credibility in the face of an unpopular war. (Photo Nixon Library)

a strong enough South Vietnam capable of at least holding its own against the North once the Americans had left, Hanoi would find itself stalemated on the battlefield. Moreover, the prospect of a stronger and more powerful South Vietnamese military might even push the North Vietnamese leadership to seek a more rapid bargain before it lost its military leverage so Kissinger reasoned.[4] To that end, massive U.S. military assistance flowed into the country creating one of the largest and best equipped militaries in the world by 1972 that would boast over a million men under arms, more than 1,000 aircraft, and 1,680 naval craft.[5]

To further tip the scales in Saigon's favor, the Nixon administration and its South Vietnamese allies launched major ground incursions into Cambodia in 1970 and into Laos in 1971 that were accompanied by increased U.S. bombing. Both operations were designed to eliminate communist cross-border sanctuaries, destroy supplies and logistics infrastructure, and disrupt enemy operational planning to buy time for Vietnamization to take hold. While the joint U.S.–South Vietnamese incursion into Cambodia in April 1970 proved highly successful in achieving many of these objectives, the South Vietnamese effort in southern Laos a year later in February and March proved to be much more of a mixed bag. Nonetheless, these ground incursions combined with the intense, ongoing American air interdiction campaign against the Ho Chi Minh Trail were responsible for the air of optimism that filled the corridors of MACV as the U.S. troop withdrawal continued on pace.

Still, many questions remained unanswered. While significant progress had been made in the arming and training of South Vietnamese forces, the quality of many of the new units remained suspect as widespread corruption, intense personal rivalries, and poor leadership hindered the development of an effective and professional officer cadre. Maintaining and servicing this new war machine without extensive U.S. assistance was also problematic given the South Vietnamese shortfall in technical and logistical capabilities. Likewise, an over-reliance on American firepower support to come to the rescue of beleaguered ARVN units created a level of dependence and unrealistic expectations that was all but impossible to maintain as Washington drew down its forces. All these factors caused many to quietly worry about the ability of Saigon's forces to effectively blunt a major North Vietnamese offensive, but there was little alternative: Vietnamization of the war was now the only game in town.

Operation Lam Son 719

The first major test of Vietnamization came in early February 1971 when South Vietnamese forces launched Operation Lam Son 719—a major effort by 16,000 troops to capture a key North Vietnamese logistic hub in southern Laos and disrupt the flow of men and supplies onto the southern battlefield—that with the exception of American air support, Saigon's forces would be operating entirely on their own for the first time.

The American-designed plan called for a heavily equipped armored and infantry column—spearheaded by the ARVN's 1st Armored Brigade's M41 Walker Bulldog tanks—to make a quick thrust up Route 9 some 25 miles into Laos to capture the town of Tchepone and destroy or capture large stockpiles of supplies there. Once this phase was complete, the attacking force would turn southwest and disrupt communist activity as it exited back across the border. To support the main column's advance and protect its flanks, thousands of troops would be airlifted by American helicopters into newly established firebases and defensive positions along the ridge lines and mountains north and south of the planned

South Vietnamese lack of coordination, poor command and control, and overly ambitious objectives proved too much to overcome during Operation Lam Son 719. (Photo National Museum of the U.S. Air Force)

route of advance. U.S. air strikes would be used to help clear the line of advance and provide close air support as needed.

Things began to go awry from the start. Highly compartmentalized and poorly coordinated planning gave troops little time to prepare. The integration of ARVN, Ranger, Airborne, and Marine units into a single composite attacking force complicated command and control problems and inflamed personal animosities across services. Moreover, the slow pace of the advance up Route 9 once the operation kicked off on February 7 gave the North Vietnamese time to mobilize their forces. After advancing only 12 miles in four days the armored column bogged down as confusion and indecision reigned and was soon forced to dig in the face of increasingly stiff enemy resistance and artillery bombardment. Value time was being lost.

Meanwhile, the communists continued to mobilize their forces, bringing elements of three North Vietnamese divisions, or upward of 36,000 men, to the fight by March. The Ranger fire support bases protecting the northern flank were the first to fall to this onslaught in late February. Soon the counterattacking enemy—now armed with heavy artillery and tanks—was threatening to completely overrun the now reeling South Vietnamese forces. The Americans responded with unrelenting air strikes that killed thousands of the enemy, but poor coordination, confusion on the ground, and lack of effective tactical control hindered their effectiveness.

As the situation deteriorated and South Vietnamese casualties mounted, President Thieu ordered the operation scaled back after the symbolic capture of Tchepone on March 6 by two airlifted battalions of the 1st ARVN Division. Finding little, but the bodies of enemy soldiers killed in pre-assault air strikes, the town was abandoned after a few days. All South Vietnamese forces began a general withdrawal from Laos on March 9 with the armored column forced to run a gauntlet of ambushes along Route 9, losing dozens of tanks and armored personnel carriers in process. By the end of the month nearly all of Saigon's troops were out and the 45-day operation was officially declared over on April 6.

Both sides claimed victory, Thieu boasting that it "was the biggest victory ever ... a moral, political and psychological Dien Bien Phu" in which more than 13,000 North Vietnamese were killed at the cost of fewer than 6,000 South Vietnamese casualties. U.S. figures indicated that Saigon lost more than 9,000 killed, wounded or captured, but the White House still portrayed the operation as a qualified success by claiming it blunted a planned North Vietnamese offensive in 1971 by destroying thousands of tons of munitions and supplies. Hanoi for its part, claimed to have inflicted more than 16,000 casualties, destroyed or captured hundreds of tanks and vehicles, and shot down hundreds of American helicopters and planes in repelling the invading force. Even more important, both sides would walk away with vastly different implications for the future of the war—ones that would have a direct bearing on the course of the 1972 Easter Offensive.

Source: D. Fulghum and T. Maitland, *South Vietnam on Trial*, pp. 68-91.

Perception is Reality

Even as the war continued to drag on amid the slow pace of peace talks in Paris, both Washington and Hanoi were moving independently along what each saw as a successful path for finally resolving the conflict in their favor. Each increasingly believed that 1972 was shaping up as a time of reckoning as their endgame strategies were reaching critical turning points. There was no going back now. Something had to give.

Despite the nagging concerns over Vietnamization, especially in light of the problems highlighted during Operation Lam Son 719, the Nixon administration had little choice but to press on. American troops were leaving South Vietnam and it was viewed as the only viable U.S. disengagement strategy in light of the strong anti-war sentiment facing the administration at home. Moreover, Nixon had campaigned in 1968 on bringing the war to an end and with another presidential election approaching he was increasingly motivated to wash his hands of Vietnam. Nonetheless, because the price of failing to obtain "peace with honor" was too high a political cost to incur, simply walking away was not an option. Moreover, the future credibility of American foreign policy and global leadership was at stake. Any resolution of the conflict in Vietnam that damaged or negatively affected American standing in the world was unacceptable. Both Nixon and Kissinger saw themselves as operating on a global stage beyond Southeast Asia: détente with the Soviet Union, arms control, revamping the Sino-American relationship, and stemming conflict

South Vietnamese troops pose with a captured North Vietnamese anti-aircraft gun during the 1970 incursion into Cambodia. (Photo National Museum of the U.S. Air Force)

in the Middle East were the new priorities for the Nixon White House. Cold, hard political calculus revealed that American military disengagement was a foregone conclusion. It was only a question of the manner and the timing of that disengagement. It would be a supreme test of wills between Washington and Hanoi, but one that Nixon and Kissinger believed they would ultimately win as long as they stayed the course on Vietnamization.

The role of international diplomacy and American grand strategy was also seen as critical in pressuring Hanoi into making concessions. By leveraging the prospect of improving relations with the Moscow and Beijing, the Nixon administration sought to isolate North Vietnam. The loss of Soviet or Chinese support—or even the perception of pending loss—might be just enough to force Hanoi's hand at the peace talks. Moreover, a closer American relationship with either benefactor would likely reduce the chances of a strident reaction from Moscow or Beijing should the United States choose to unleash massive military force directly against the North Vietnamese. While high-profile American summit diplomacy failed to break the negotiation logjam in early 1972, the message was clearly not lost on Hanoi: old alliances are vulnerable, as the world is changing.

But in order for the American strategy to work, Washington would have to rely on tailored military action to affirm its political resolve to stay the course in seeking a negotiated

In Lam Son 719—a bold, but ill-fated 1971 incursion into southern Laos—Saigon's forces not only failed to disrupt the North Vietnamese military buildup there, but the operation highlighted glaring weaknesses in the Vietnamization process. (Photo National Museum of the U.S. Air Force)

The Stalled Paris Peace Talks

Although peace talks between American and North Vietnamese officials had been ongoing since May 1968, little progress had been made by 1972 as neither Washington nor Hanoi was ready to make the necessary concessions to advance the cause of peace or candidly admit that a military solution was beyond reach. Entrenched positions, such as Hanoi's demand for the removal of South Vietnamese President Nguyen Van Thieu or Washington's requirement that all North Vietnamese troops leave the South, left little room for compromise. Moreover, both sides continued to pursue dual-track strategies of seeking a military advantage on the battlefield to buttress their position at the bargaining table: the Nixon administration believed that Vietnamization would push Hanoi to seek a deal with Washington rather than be faced with the prospect of dealing with a strengthened, U.S.-supported regime in Saigon once American troops left the country, while First Secretary Le Duan and his politburo allies believed that one final military push just might be enough to topple the Thieu government, forcing Washington to accept Hanoi's terms or face the prospect of returning to the battlefield.

Pressure, however, was mounting behind the scenes for both sides to reach a compromise sooner rather than later. Strong anti-war sentiment in the United States and growing U.S. congressional restrictions on war operations and funding, as well as the drawdown in American forces, greatly constrained President Nixon's ability to threaten Hanoi. Nagging concerns by U.S. military advisers and some White House officials over the ability of South Vietnamese forces to stand on their own put the ultimate success of the U.S. Vietnamization strategy in doubt. And despite President Thieu's re-election in 1971, the Saigon regime remained as divide, fragile, and unpopular as ever. The picture wasn't much better for Hanoi either. The American policy of détente with the Soviet Union and rapprochement with China made the North increasing vulnerable to the broader foreign policy agendas of Moscow and Beijing. Even more disconcerting, the widening Sino-Soviet split forced Hanoi to strike a delicate political balance or face a potential cut-off in vital sources of military assistance. Although still welding a firm hand over the party in the wake of Ho Chi Minh's death in 1969, Le Duan and his allies were on shaky ground. Repeated efforts to foment a popular uprising in the South through protracted warfare had failed to take root and the Viet Cong insurgency had yet to recover from its mauling during the 1968 Tet Offensive.

Not surprisingly both Hanoi and Washington would seek once more during 1972 to use military force to break the deadlock and bring about a favorable resolution to the war. More so than at any other time in the talks, the final nine months of the year would be a turning point. Miscalculation combined with military desperation would push each to the brink. Wide swings of euphoria and despair would engulf both sides before ultimately the pressure not to make peace—even if it was only the illusion of peace—became too much to bear for each side. But first events on the battlefield would have to play out.

settlement and for its continued support to the Thieu government. However, as American ground combat forces continued their steadily decline and U.S. congressional war restrictions increased, the Nixon administration found itself almost entirely dependent on air power to accomplish these objectives. But would air power alone be enough? And what if Hanoi sought to take advantage of the declining American military position to improve its own position at the bargaining table? Thus, Nixon and Kissinger were taking a huge and dangerous risk, but it was one that the White House felt it couldn't avoid not to make.

For the most part the gamble appeared to be paying off at the start of 1972. The bombing of Cambodia and the intense three-year, aerial interdiction effort in southern Laos (known as Operation Commando Hunt) not only signaled continuing American resolve, but was also apparently successful in at least slowing the flow of men and matériel onto the southern battleground. Although controversy surrounded the extent of Commando Hunt's success—with the CIA low-balling Air Force claims—the Joint Chiefs of Staff believed that any "hampering of the flow of men and supplies ... greatly restricted enemy initiatives and in some cases forced him to forego planned operations."[6] Moreover, to maintain and defend this vital logistics pipeline the North Vietnamese were increasingly forced to divert more and more resources, deploying almost 100,000 laborers and troops to the Lao panhandle by 1972.[7]

Likewise, the rising use of preemptive air strikes by Washington against the North Vietnamese military buildup in the country's southern panhandle just across the demilitarized zone (DMZ) was a cost-effective way of maintain U.S. negotiating leverage and also buying time for Vietnamization to work. Officially known as "protective reaction strikes," these missions were characterized as defensive and retaliatory in nature, but they soon evolved into a de facto bombing campaign as the frequency and intensity increased. The first three months of 1972 saw more than 90 protective reaction strikes launched (compared to 108 during all of the previous year),[8] as North Vietnamese air defenses,

Le Duc Tho and Henry Kissinger struggled throughout 1970 and 1971 to negotiate a diplomatic solution to the war that both their respective governments would find acceptable.

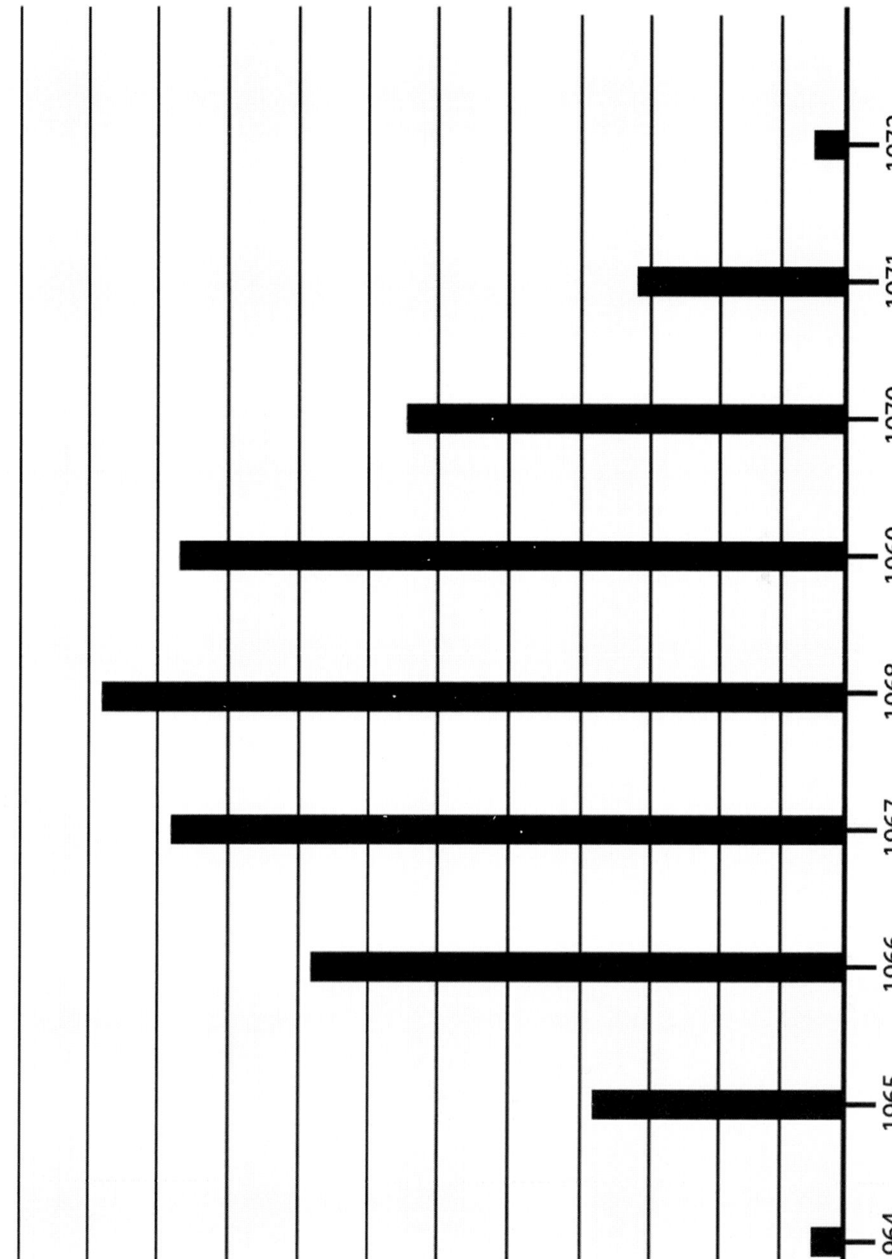

Graph 1: U.S. Troop Levels, 1964–1972

oil storage and supply depots, and troop concentrations were increasingly targeted. The Americans were sending a forceful message: Hanoi should not seek to take advantage of the U.S. military drawdown in the South, because Washington was more than willing to escalate the bombing if necessary. The message, however, was largely ignored, because Hanoi was operating under its own political-military calculus that required a testing of the limits of American resolve and capability.

Now it seemed that the stars were beginning to align to put that plan into action. With Nixon facing re-election in the face of an unpopular war, North Vietnamese leaders reasoned that his hands would be increasingly tied by domestic political considerations. Likewise, the White House's public commitment to de-escalating the war through troop withdrawals and the dwindling size of U.S. combat forces in Vietnam would likely limit Washington's ability to respond militarily. And even if the Americans resumed widespread bombing of the North as they had repeatedly threatened, the North Vietnamese had weathered the storm before during Operation Rolling Thunder and could do it again. Besides the Soviets and Chinese were likely to denounce any new bombing campaign and put diplomatic pressure on the Americans to stop it.

Militarily, things were looking up for Hanoi too. Its forces and logistics networks in Cambodia and southern Laos had not only been reconstituted, but they were more expansive than ever. Most critically, the poor performance of Saigon's forces during Lam Son 719 not only boosted the confidence of the North Vietnamese Army (NVA) in its ability to go toe to toe with the best the South Vietnamese had to offer and win, but it validated Hanoi's belief in the failure of Vietnamization.[9] Not surprisingly then, in mid-1971 the politburo of the North Vietnamese communist party determined that "the time has come to bring about a favorable moment" and "intensify our struggle [through military action to] achieve a decisive victory in the year 1972 and compel the American imperialists to end the war through negotiations on our terms."[10] Accordingly, military planning for a general offensive—along the lines of the 1968 Tet Offensive—to strike a crushing blow against the Saigon government kicked into high gear.

Thus, the day of reckoning was fast approaching for both Washington and Hanoi with each believing that they held the upper hand; with just a little more effort their strategy would open the door to victory—either on the battlefield or at the negotiating table—but either way a collision of monumental proportions was in the offing.

Hanoi Rolls the Dice

As early as March 1971, communist logistics support units in the border regions were told to prepare for an extensive military campaign that might "decide the war,"[11] but these preparations took on new urgency in the waning months of 1971 and into early 1972 as the North pushed tens of thousands of men and massive amounts of military equipment and supplies southward. Ultimately, Hanoi would be able to amass upwards of 225,000 men along the South Vietnamese border stretching from the DMZ to Cambodian border north of Saigon. This formidable armada included armored personnel carriers, hundreds of light PT-76 and medium T-54/55 tanks, and dozens of long-range 122-mm and 130-mm artillery pieces, as well as huge 160-mm mortars that were part of the roughly $1.5 billion in military aid received from the Soviet Union and China over the past two years.[12] Air defense would be provided by self-propelled ZSU-57 anti-aircraft guns, as well as large numbers of newly arrived, handheld SA-7 surface-to-air missiles.

The volume of supplies moving down the Ho Chi Minh Trail doubled in 1971 as Transportation Group 559 pushed matériel southward with its fleet of 8,000 trucks[13] and soon stockpiles of food, ammunition, and fuel were overflowing rear depot areas of Cambodia and Laos. Likewise, an extensive campaign road network extending all the way along the frontier was put in place to facilitate movement by NVA mechanized units heading south. One unit, the 171st Tank Battalion, traveled more than 750 miles from its base in North Vietnam along this network, undergoing numerous air attacks over the course of two months, to arrive at its starting position on the border northwest of Saigon with 97 percent of vehicles intact.[14] According to the official North Vietnamese military history, "there was an excited atmosphere of advancing into battle" not seen since the heady early days of the war.[15]

The operational plan was just as bold: a coordinated three-pronged, cross-border thrust into the northern, central, and southern regions of South Vietnam that was designed to grind down enemy forces and push Saigon's military to point of implosion while seizing large swaths of territory south of the DMZ. This conventional NVA assault would be complemented by a general uprising across the country's interior by Viet Cong guerrillas and newly infiltrated North Vietnamese cadres to further disrupt and destabilize the Thieu government. Although not designed to administer a coup de grâce, the powerful North Vietnamese Secretary General Le Duan and his party allies certainly saw victory on the battlefield as irrevocably altering the strategic landscape of the war and sowing the

By 1972 Hanoi had modernized its military into a conventional fighting force equipped with hundreds of tanks, heavy artillery pieces, and mobile anti-aircraft weapons.

seeds for ultimate victory at the peace table. If the offensive was successful it would thoroughly discredit Vietnamization. It would further fuel the American anti-war movement and undermine the Nixon administration's ability to negotiate. Moreover, it dovetailed with their current talk-fight strategy that would allow Hanoi to seek political concessions at the peace talks from an increased position of military strength on the southern battlefield.

Nonetheless, victory was far from assured. Even a weakened South Vietnamese foe could still likely count on strong American support. Even more critically, for the first time the North Vietnamese would be relying on a conventional ground assault using unproven combined arms tactics to achieve a decisive victory before the Americans could effectively respond. Time would be of the essence. In addition, this new type of warfare required an effective and functioning logistics network that ran all the way from Hanoi and Haiphong to support ongoing combat operations on the southern battlefields. Not only would this leave the North's supply lines highly vulnerable to American air attack, but it would leave Hanoi more politically and militarily dependent than ever on the continued flow of Soviet and Chinese supplies. And although Le Duan saw a general uprising as a key component of the offensive that would disrupt the government's response and cause nationwide upheaval, the Viet Cong were in poor position to provide much assistance.

All of this, however, failed to dampen Hanoi's enthusiasm or the confidence of its military that a turning point was at hand. "We were told," one NVA officer recalled, that "this was the one time in 1,000 years that the situation would be [so] favorable for us."[16] So Hanoi rolled the dice and attacked.

The powerful Secretary General of the Vietnamese Communist party, Le Duan, pushed for a military solution to the war in 1972, rather than pursue a negotiated settlement with the Americans.

2. TO THE SOUND OF THE BUGLES

While South Vietnamese commanders and MACV had been monitoring the North Vietnamese military buildup for some time and were anticipating an attack since mid-February around the start of the Chinese new year, they were completely shocked at the sheer magnitude and breadth of the offensive, as well as the willingness of the enemy to commit large numbers of tanks, artillery, and mechanized troops to the attack. Hanoi's 1972 Easter Offensive—officially known as the Nguyen Hue Campaign[1]—would bring to bear the largest concentration of communist conventional firepower ever seen in the war and push the South Vietnamese military and its American ally to the brink. The next six months of fighting would see a desperate attempt by both sides to turn the tables on the battlefield, but ultimately Hanoi and Washington would be forced back to the negotiating table to achieve their objectives.

The Northern Onslaught Begins

At midday on March 30, 1972, the still of the jungle was broken by the rumble of tanks and the unleashing of a heavy artillery barrage against South Vietnamese outposts across northern Quang Tri Province as some 30,000 North Vietnamese soldiers from the 308th NVA Division and at least eight independent regiments surged across the DMZ and out of eastern Laos, signaling the start of the largest communist offensive since 1968. Moreover, the thrust directly across the DMZ achieved great tactical surprise, because South Vietnamese commanders believed the North would not dare blatantly flout the 1954 Geneva accords. When Lieutenant General Hoang Xuan Lam, the I Corps commander, was once asked about the possibility, he simply remarked, "They cannot."[2] But then of course they did. Over the course of the next month, three veteran infantry divisions, some two dozen independent regiments, along with at least 200 tanks, scores of heavy artillery pieces, and air defense assets would be committed to the fight in the northern two provinces of the country to test the limits of Saigon's and Washington's capabilities.

Standing in the face of this oncoming onslaught on the opening day of the offensive were some 25,000 government troops from two ARVN infantry divisions, two South Vietnamese Marine brigades, and a handful of newly activated armored and artillery units, plus an assorted mixture of local territorial troops spread across the Quang Tri and Thua Thien provinces of Military Region 1 (MR 1).[3] Not only were the odds stacked against the South Vietnamese defenders, but they occupied a series of scattered and poorly integrated outposts and fire support bases that were anchored by a few strongpoints. It was a defensive deployment designed to counter guerrilla infiltration from the North, not face a full-fledged combined arms attack. Pummeled by relentless heavy and accurate enemy artillery fire—much it coming from long-range 130-mm guns north of the DMZ—the main South Vietnamese fire support bases were unable to provide covering fire to their comrades. To compound the problem, elements of the 56th and 2d infantry regiments of

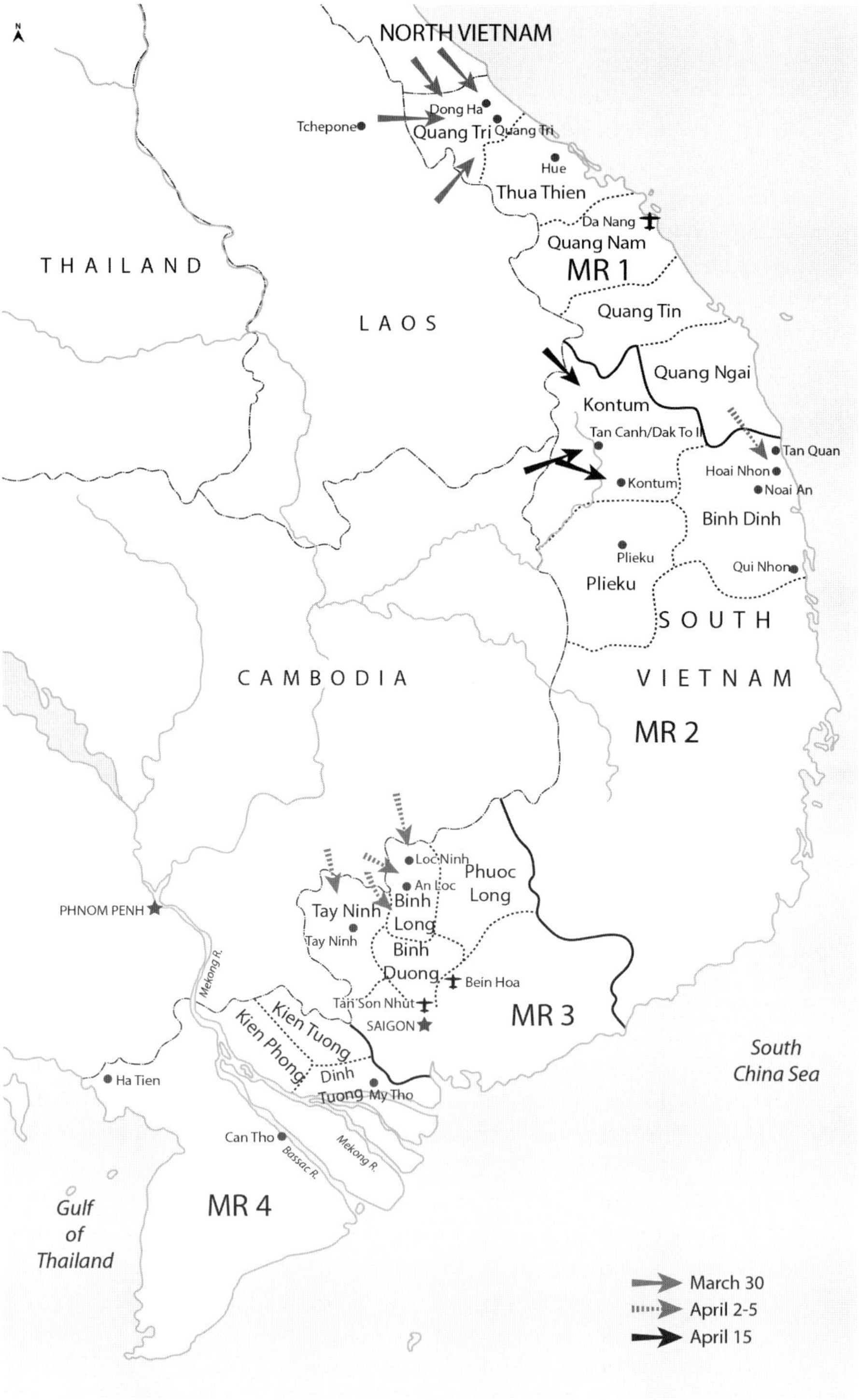

Map 2: The Opening Round.

the 3d ARVN Division were caught in the middle of a routine rotation of troops between bases on the day of the attack.

Position after government position, from the coastal plain to the western line of mountaintop fire support bases, were quickly isolated and overrun in the first 48 hours of the offensive. General Lam's so-called defensive "ring of steel" was anything but and began to crack immediately. The death knell came on April 2 with the sudden surrender of Camp Carroll—under highly suspect conditions[4]—that anchored the western end of the defenses to elements of the 308th NVA Division and the 204th Tank Regiment. Some 1,500 men of 56th ARVN Regiment along with bulk of MR 1 heavy artillery, including several massive 175-mm guns, fell into the hands of the enemy.[5] The 56th Regiment ceased to exist. The 3d Division's veteran commander, Brigadier General Vu Van Giai, was incensed. Not only had he lost one-third of his command and a key strongpoint in one fell swoop, but I Corps headquarters seemed oblivious to the seriousness of his plight.

The situation to the east along the coast was just as desperate. Soldiers of the 3d Division's 57th ARVN Regiment were falling back to the Mieu Giang and Cua Viet rivers as they unsuccessfully attempted to delay the enemy's advance down Highway 1 that Easter Sunday. Rushing to defend the critical highway bridge over the Mieu Giang at Dong Ha, some nine miles south of the DMZ, and the approaches from the west and south of the river were a battalion of South Vietnamese Marines and 44 brand-new M48A3 Patton tanks. The tanks belonged to the newly formed and untested 20th Tank Regiment, 1st Armored Brigade, that had been hurried forward from their base south of Quang Tri city. It was just in time. The Pattons quickly scored kills with their high-velocity 90-mm guns on the unsuspecting advancing enemy, leaving at least nine PT-76 and two T-54/55 tanks in flames and forcing the enemy armored column to fall back from the river.[6] But the respite was brief. Hastily scrambled South Vietnamese Air Force (VNAF) A-1 Skyraiders joined in the renewed fighting, while American advisers on the ground directed gunfire from four U.S. destroyers against repeated enemy attempts to seize the road and railway bridges spanning the river.

There was, however, only so much a handful of Marines and Patton tanks could do against a division-sized force supported by tanks. Despite General Lam's orders to preserve the highway bridge to facilitate a future counterattack, the two American advisers on scene decided to destroy it before the bridge could fall into enemy hands. If the North Vietnamese were able to cross the river in strength, they could push rapidly south along Highway 1 to Quang Tri and even all the way to Hue before any reconstituted form of resistance could be established. In a heroic display of grit and determination by Captain John Ripley and Major John Smock, the bridge was blown that afternoon. Ripley would be awarded the Navy Cross for his actions that day and go down in U.S. Marine Corps lore as single-handedly blunting the North Vietnamese attack in the opening days of the offensive. The resulting loss of the highway bridge forced the enemy armor to divert some eight miles to the west and cross the Mieu Giang River at Cam Lo, thus buying time for the defense of Quang Tri city.

While disaster had been averted for now, the front-line situation continued to deteriorate. Elements of the 304th NVA Division and the attached 203d Tank Regiment rolled

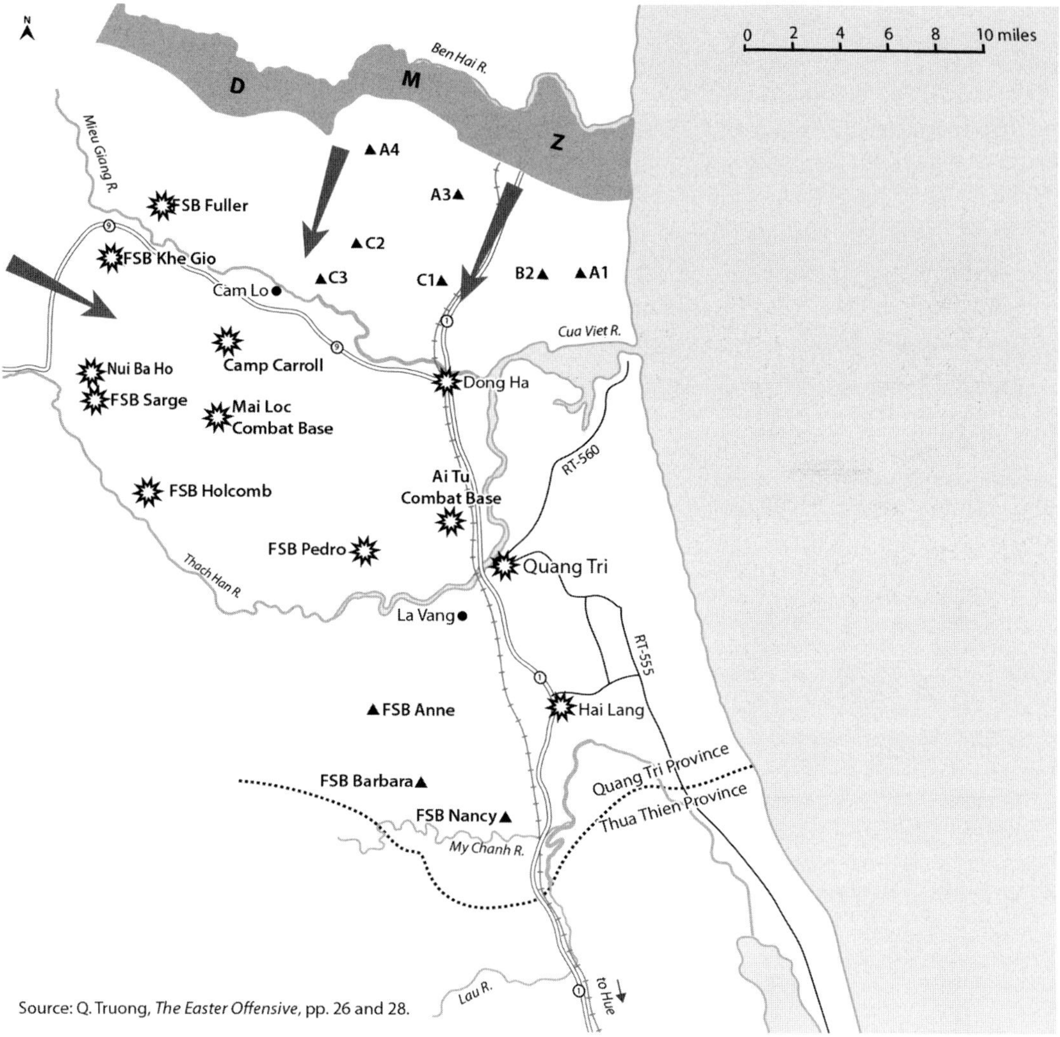

Map 3: The Battle for Military Region 1.

up the western flank of the 3d Division and began driving eastward along the south bank of the Thach Han River toward the coast. Thanks however to the timely arrival of some 9,000 reinforcements from a new Marine brigade and nine Ranger battalions released from the country's strategic reserve,[7] General Giai was able to establish a new defensive line just west of Dong Ha and Quang Tri city and paralleling Highway 1 southward to the Thach Han River by April 8.

From this new defensive position government troops, many now armed with the new American M72 light anti-tank weapons (LAWs), were able to beat back the enemy's combined infantry and armored assaults over the following days. In one ferocious battle for fire support base Pedro, west of Quang Tri city and astride Route 557, the North

President Nixon remained committed to his promise to withdraw all American combat troops from South Vietnam by pinning his hopes on the success of Vietnamization.

Vietnamese sent an entire regiment supported by some two dozen T-54/55 tanks against two Marine battalions and a handful of M48 tanks and armored personnel carriers. The fighting lasted over three days before the attackers were finally repulsed; 23 NVA tanks were either destroyed or captured and more than 420 of the enemy were killed at the cost of 66 South Vietnamese casualties.[8] While poor weather continued to hamper close air support, a steady stream of B-52 strikes by the U.S. Air Force against suspected enemy troop concentrations to the west provided a huge morale boost to the weary defenders. And the line held.

With the tactical situation stabilizing, the arrival of additional reinforcements, and clearing weather, General Lam began calling for a counteroffensive to turn the tide of battle. Lam's ambitious plan, Operation Quang Trung 729,[9] called for an all-out attack to the west beginning on April 14 to recapture Cam Lo, Camp Carroll, and Mai Loc and reestablish the former defensive line. Although the improved weather allowed American and VNAF tactical aircraft to pummel forward North Vietnamese positions, the counter-offensive never had a chance of success. A convoluted and disorganized operational chain of command, I Corps headquarters interference, and coordination problems plagued the operation from the start. Moreover, Saigon's physically weary and mentally exhausted troops were in no mood to advance in the face of stiff resistance. By April 17 none of the attacking troops had advanced more than a half-mile from their starting positions. Thus, rather than turning the tide of battle for the Saigon government, the fighting devolved into "a costly battle of attrition in which the ARVN forces were steadily reduced in strength and effectiveness by the enemy's deadly artillery fire," according to a senior American adviser.[10]

Meanwhile, Hanoi showed no signs of backing down. Not only did it continue to pour additional troops, armor, artillery, and air defense units—including the first ever deployment of SA-2 surface-to-air missiles inside South Vietnam—onto the northern battlefield in the final weeks of April, but it increased the pressure on two other fronts as well. Saigon may have weathered the initial onslaught in the north, but the worst had yet to come.

Hanoi's Opening Moves in the South

Months prior to the outbreak of fighting in the north, South Vietnamese intelligence became aware of a steady buildup and repositioning of communist forces along the Cambodian border opposite Binh Long and Tay Ninh provinces that lay to the north of Saigon. What was unclear, however, was the enemy's intent, especially once the Easter Offensive kicked off on March 30. Some saw the southern buildup as a prelude to a major thrust toward Saigon, while others believed any attack would be diversionary in nature to tie down government forces and prevent the release of reinforcements to the northern battlefield.[11] Either way, the III Corps commander, Lieutenant General Nguyen Van Minh, and his troops were woefully unprepared for what was about to befall them over the next several months.

Lieutenant General Hoang Xuan Lam, I Corps commander, struggled to mount an effective defense of Quang Tri Province at the onset of the North Vietnamese offensive.

General Minh's some 40,000 troops were responsible for the defense of the eleven provinces of Military Region 3 (MR 3) that also encompassed Saigon, but the bulk of his forces were arrayed near or along the Cambodian frontier and had been heavily involved in cross-border operations under Minh's predecessor. By 1972, however, III Corps had opted for a more passive, in-depth defensive strategy that consisted of a series of frontier outposts, fire support bases, and strongpoints that was designed to delay rather than prevent an attack. With the 25th ARVN Division's headquarters and reserves concentrated in the provincial capital of Tay Ninh and the 5th ARVN Division headquarters and reserves at Lai Khe in northern Binh Duong Province, significant forces could then respond quickly to any enemy cross-border incursion. While fine in theory, this approach allowed the North Vietnamese and Viet Cong to mass their troops and equipment

The scope and intensity of the North Vietnamese attack across three military regions in its opening weeks caught the South Vietnamese ill-prepared to cope with a such an onslaught.

unfettered on the Cambodian side of the border, as well as choose the time and place of any future attack. It was a situation that Hanoi would be all too happy to exploit during the upcoming offensive.

In the early morning hours of April 2, 1972, amid the confusion in the north, fighting broke out in Tay Ninh Province when the 24th NVA Regiment supported by tanks assaulted and quickly overran the ARVN fire support base at Lac Long on the Cambodian border. Several other frontier outposts were soon captured, while others were simply abandoned as III Corp headquarters ordered outlying elements of the 25th Division to fall back on Tay Ninh city and establish a defensive perimeter. During the withdrawal several ARVN battalions were ambushed, suffering heavy casualties and forced to abandon their vehicles and artillery as they retreated. This was just the beginning. Over the coming weeks, Hanoi would send three full divisions, two independent regiments, and armor and artillery pouring across the border. But Tay Ninh city was not the objective of the campaign, as MR 3 commanders were about to find out.

The real center of gravity for the North Vietnamese assault was neighboring Long Binh Province. It was here that they hoped to seize large chucks of territory, as well as the provincial capital of An Loc in the hope of establishing a Viet Cong provincial government there. If successful, this phase of the Nguyen Hue Campaign would not only produce a major psychological victory for the communists, but it would likely destroy large numbers of South Vietnamese troops and in the process eviscerate Washington's Vietnamization strategy.

Some 12 miles from the border, the ARVN garrison at Loc Ninh sat astride Route 13 and was the first objective of Lieutenant General Tran Van Tra's attack on Binh Long Province.

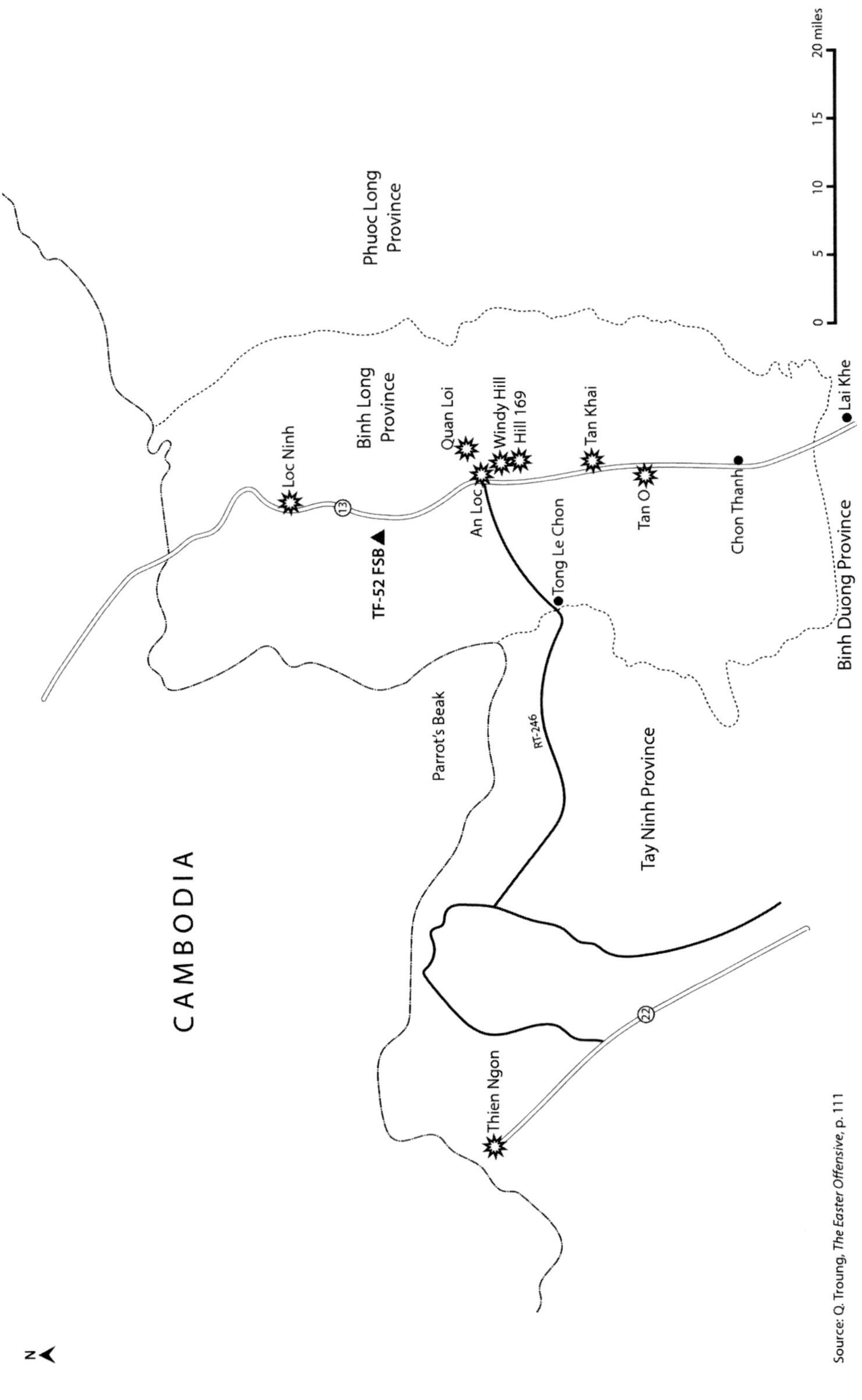

Source: Q. Troung, *The Easter Offensive*, p. 111

Map 4: The Battle for Military Region 3.

North Vietnamese commanders made highly effective use of their long-range 130-mm and 122-mm artillery to pummel South Vietnamese defenses in advance of infantry assaults.

Pushing rapidly southward across the frontier on April 4, the 5th NVA/VC Division, supported by two companies of the 203d Tank Regiment and long-range 130-mm artillery, steamrolled toward the city. A squadron of the ARVN 1st Armored Regiment and two supporting infantry battalions were caught by surprise while retreating toward Loc Ninh and decimated; the North Vietnamese claiming 1,400 enemy troops killed or wounded, 52 vehicles destroyed, and 12 tanks captured.[12]

By the next day, the 9th Regiment of the 5th ARVN Division and its team of seven American advisers at Loc Ninh found themselves under a full-scale armored and artillery assault. Relying on massive doses of close air support called in by the Americans and by circling forward air controllers (FACs), the attackers were kept at bay throughout the next 24 hours. A constant stream of American-piloted A-37 Dragonfly fighter-bombers of the 8th Special Operations Squadron flying out of Bien Hoa air base wreaked havoc on attacking enemy tanks, while orbiting Air Force AC-130 Spectre gunships turned back repeated infantry charges. Still it wouldn't be enough. Panic soon took hold of the outnumbered defenders as the day wore on. Ammunition ran low and command broke down completely as all organized resistance crumbled. The garrison fell on the morning of April 7 with the North Vietnamese reportedly taking some 1,300 ARVN prisoners and capturing two batteries of 105-mm and 155-mm howitzers.[13] Only a handful of survivors would eventually reach the safety of An Loc and all seven American advisers were listed as missing in action.[14]

Meanwhile, an ARVN battalion from a 5th Division task force advancing toward Loc Ninh was ambushed by the 209th Infantry Regiment, 9th NVA/VC Division, and badly mauled some six miles south of the city. The remainder of the 1,000-man task force also soon found itself under heavy and unrelenting North Vietnamese attack as it withdrew south along Route 13. In the ensuing chaos the troops were forced to abandon much of their equipment, including artillery and armored personnel carriers, and flee into the jungle. General Tra had won the first round and now the provincial capital of An Loc appeared ripe for the picking as he moved his troops into position to encircle of the city.

Sporadic fighting around An Loc had already begun well prior to the fall of Loc Ninh as the enemy pushed ever closer and outlying South Vietnamese units fell back toward the city. Late on the evening of April 7 the airstrip and high ground just east of An Loc were overrun. Then a regiment of the 7th NVA/VC Division took up a blocking position at Tan Khai about ten miles south of An Loc, thus completing the isolation of the city. It was here at Tan Khai on April 11 that III Corps reserves from the 1st Airborne Brigade advancing up Route 13 encountered stiff resistance and were halted in their tracks.

The defenders of An Loc were now entirely dependent on airlift for reinforcements and supplies, forcing the big C-130 transports of the 374th Tactical Airlift Wing (TAW) out of Bien Hoa into service. Over the course of several days, two battalions of the 8th Regiment, 5th ARVN Division, along with two battalions from the 3d Ranger Group were uplifted by helicopters from the 1st U.S. Cavalry Division—one of the few remaining American combat units left in country. The 1st Cav would also begin a round-the-clock effort to ferry in supplies to assist the 374th TAW. Knowing this, the North Vietnamese moved increasing numbers of anti-aircraft weapons, including new, man-portable SA-7s, onto the battlefield

Saigon's network of often isolated and unsupported fire support bases became easy prey to waves of attacking enemy troops.

South Vietnamese A-37B Dragonfly ground attack aircraft played a critical role in the defense of Binh Long Province in the opening weeks of the offensive.

to cut off the aerial lifeline. Their efforts would take a deadly toll not only on the low- and slow-flying helicopters and FACs, but also account for the shooting down of three C-130Es and one AC-119K in April and May.[15] The siege of An Loc was on.

While neither the Americans nor South Vietnamese expected to fight a major battle at An Loc—let alone one with such serious implications—they had little choice as the psychological loss of a provincial capital just 50 miles northwest of Saigon was unacceptable, because it would shake the Thieu government to its core, expose the frailty of Vietnamization, and seriously undermine Washington's negotiating position in Paris.

Nonetheless, the defense of the city was makeshift at best. Brigadier General Le Van Hung, the 5th Division commander, hastily sought to fortify his perimeter and cobble together his 3,000 fresh troops with 1,300 Rangers, the remnants of his battered forces from the north, and about 2,000 territorial militiamen. They were supported by a handful of surviving 105-mm and 155-mm artillery pieces. In all, the South Vietnamese garrison numbered approximately 7,500 men.[16] General Hung was assisted in the defense of the city by U.S Army Colonel William Miller and some two dozen other American advisers, many of whom were embedded with South Vietnamese units. The U.S. advisers' role in the coming battle would prove to be pivotal in both terms of military acumen and morale.

For their part, the North Vietnamese would mass the better part of three infantry divisions—spearheaded by the 9th NVA/VC Division—along with an artillery division, elements of two tank regiments, and supporting units, totaling about 21,000 men.[17] The attackers also had a massive advantage in armor and artillery over the defenders, but would find themselves subject to unrelenting American and South Vietnamese air strikes over the course of the siege. Highly confident of success, "the word among North Vietnamese was that An Loc would fall by April 20."[18]

From the night of April 12 the enemy shelling intensified to the point that "not a single square meter of An Loc was free of impacts from 82-mm mortars, 122-mm rockets, 130-mm guns, and also from [captured] 105-mm and 155-mm howitzers," according to one South Vietnamese officer.[19] The first waves of North Vietnamese infantry from the 9th Division's 271st and 272d regiments that were supported by tanks and other armored vehicles from the 203d Tank Regiment struck the northeast defenses in the early morning of April 13. Heavy defensive fire and near constant tactical air strikes called in by Colonel Miller took their toll on the attackers, but several T-54/55 tanks were able to penetrate well into the city. Unsupported by infantry, however, the isolated tanks soon fell prey to South Vietnamese soldiers armed with M72 anti-tank rockets. Undaunted, the enemy continued to press its attacks over the next two days, suffering close to 1,000 casualties and losing at least 23 tanks in the process, but was able to establish a foothold in the northern part of the city.[20]

Although the situation was still desperate, the defenders of An Loc had weathered the initial storm and reinforcements were reportedly on the way. A battalion of 1st Airborne Brigade had just been airlifted into the battle to secure key hills less than two miles southeast of the city and with the help of American AH-1 Cobra gunships drove the North Vietnamese from the position after desperate hand-to-hand fighting. Meanwhile, the newly redeployed 21st ARVN Division had arrived from the Mekong Delta and was preparing to move north from its position at Chon Thanh and break the siege. All this as B-52 heavy bombers continued to unleash their deadly payloads within a half mile of friendly positions, orbiting gunships blasted enemy troop concentrations, and tactical air strikes hammered tanks and the enemy's supply lines. Major General James Hollingsworth, the senior U.S. adviser to General Minh at III Corps, was brimming

South Vietnam President Nguyen Van Thieu's predilection for placing politically supportive generals in senior command positions would nearly prove to be his government's undoing. (Photo Naval History and Historical Command)

with confidence. "The enemy hit us hard all day long with everything he could muster—and we threw it right back at him."[21] Well, at least for now.

After a brief two-day lull, the North Vietnamese launched an intense artillery and rocket barrage early on April 19 with over 1,000 rounds slamming into the city. But instead of assaulting the city directly, the enemy sent two regiments to dislodge the ARVN paratroops on hills to the southeast and soon overran them despite strong resistance. Now able to position artillery on the dominating high ground, the North Vietnamese launched their assault on the city itself, but they were repeatedly repulsed in savage house-to-house fighting. A series of well-coordinated tactical air strikes also prevented the 9th Division commander from reinforcing and resupplying his frontline troops. Furthermore, an attempted North Vietnamese flanking movement to attack from the south of the city up Route 13 on April 21 was stymied by the timely arrival of two battalions of the 1st Airborne Brigade. Suffering heavy losses in men—an estimated 2,000 from bombing alone over the past week[22]—and matériel, the North Vietnamese assault ground to a halt on April 23, as both sides welcomed the respite to take stock of the situation.

The Central Highlands Come Under Attack

Even before the fierce fighting at An Loc commenced, the long anticipated North Vietnamese assault on Military Region 2 (MR 2) began—but not where anyone initially expected. While there had been extensive skirmishing along the frontier for months, with several major probes recently launched against western ARVN outposts—provoking American B-52 Arc Light strikes on enemy staging areas along the Cambodian and Lao border—the first attacks in MR 2 took place in the coastal province of Binh Dinh. On April 5 the veteran NT-3 "Gold Star" Division augmented by local Viet Cong forces burst out the An Lao River valley, quickly overwhelming ARVN and local defense forces in the province's two northern districts. With the help of several thousand additional North Vietnamese reinforcements infiltrated through Quang Ngai Province, the attackers then pushed south and east toward Hoai Nhon, Hoai An, and the vitally important Highway 1.

Facing the brunt of this assault was the 40th Regiment of the 22d ARVN Division, which senior American adviser John Paul Vann had urged II Corps commander, Lieutenant General Ngo Dzu, to keep in place for such an eventuality. Nonetheless, the defenders seemed ill-prepared and quickly became demoralized under weak command leadership. Try as they might though, the American advisers in Binh Dinh Province had little success in cajoling or even browbeating unit commanders to stand and fight. Position after position was abandoned, often with little to no resistance. Soon the town of Hoai An came under heavy rocket and mortar fire as the enemy closed in. A planned orderly withdrawn, however, succumbed to panic as troops and their families fled pell-mell toward Landing Zone English, the last surviving major ARVN defensive position in the northern half of the province. Now with his lines of communications to the west increasingly threatened, General Dzu was facing a dilemma as whether to send reinforcements to defend Binh Dinh Province while anticipating a major enemy thrust against the Central Highlands.

The decision would be made for him when Major General Hoang Minh Thai launched the third prong of the Easter Offensive on April 12. The full weight of 320th NVA Division

Airborne troops rush to the defense of An Loc in mid-April 1972.

was thrown against a string of fire support bases held by the 2nd Airborne Brigade atop "Rocket Ridge," the strategic high ground lying just southwest of Tan Canh and screening the Route 14 link to Kontum. The badly outnumbered paratroopers and Rangers fought desperately to stem the tide amid unrelenting North Vietnamese artillery and mortar fire that masked repeated infantry charges. American advisers at the fire support bases directed wave after wave of friendly aircraft against the advancing enemy with devastating effect. But once again it wasn't enough. Position after position was overrun or abandoned; the final fire base fell on April 21, thus, breaching General Dzu's main defensive line.

Meanwhile to the north, on April 19, nearly 20,000 troops from the 2d NVA Division, the better part of four independent regiments, and tanks from 203d Tank Regiment moved out of their Laotian staging areas to complete the envelopment of the 22d ARVN Division's battalions defending the Central Highlands. Soon the enemy was hammering the ARVN garrisons at Tan Canh and Dak To II with heavy 130-mm artillery and 122-mm rocket fire in preparation for a full-scale assault. With only some 2,000 men, a few batteries of 155-mm and 105-mm howitzers, and a handful of dug-in M41 tanks and armored personnel carriers, the situation looked increasingly bleak for the two cutoff garrisons. Colonel Le Duc Dat, the 22d Division commander at Tan Canh, grew despondent and demoralized. "We're going to lose, we're going to be overrun, we will all be killed or captured," he told his American adviser.[23]

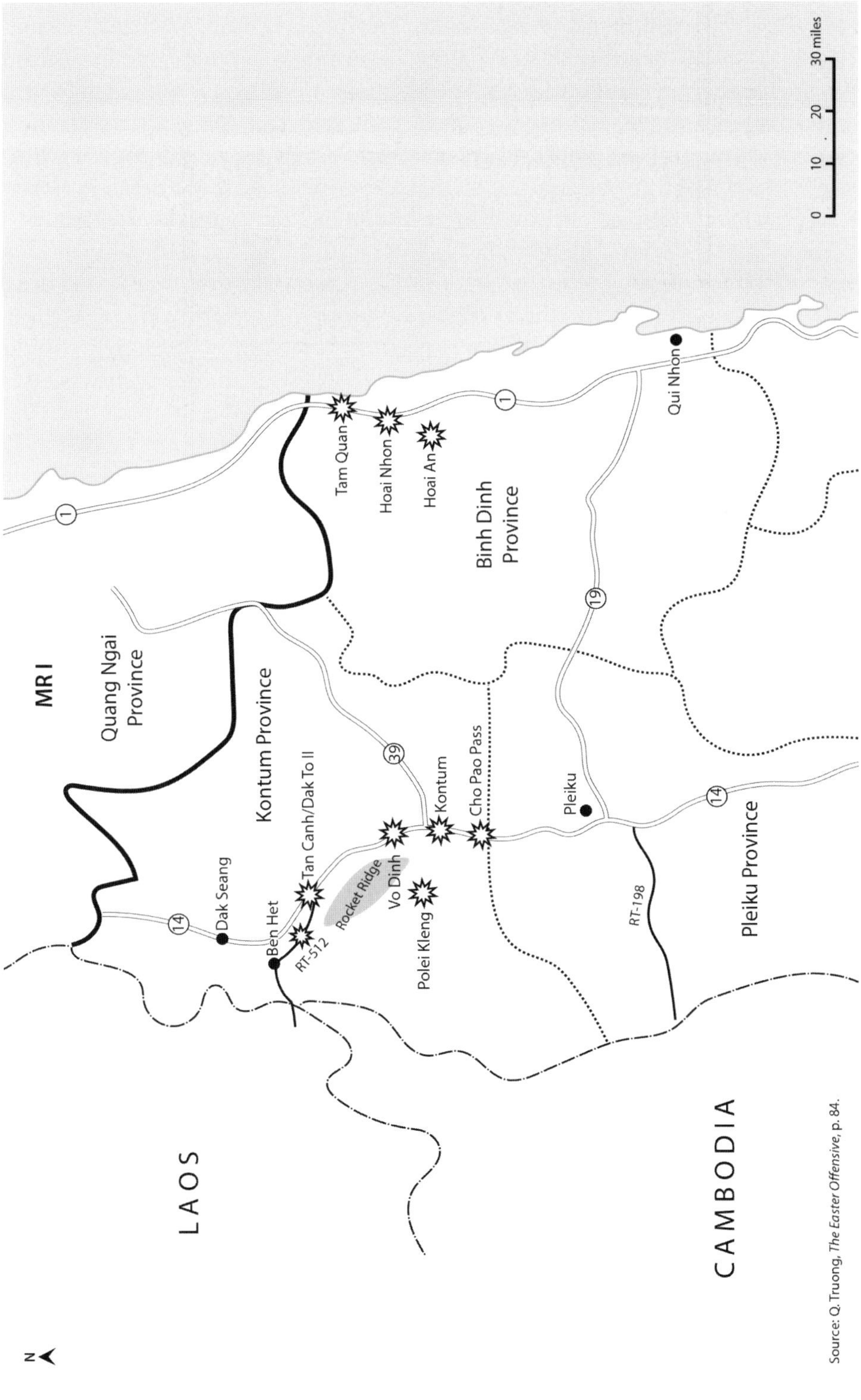

Source: Q. Truong, *The Easter Offensive*, p. 84.

Map 5: The Battle for Military Region 2.

On April 23, the 66th Independent Infantry Regiment and the 2d NVA Division's 1st Regiment slammed into Tan Canh. As T-54/55 tanks smashed through the perimeter wire terrorizing the defenders, masses of enemy infantry followed, disabling M41 tanks and defensive bunkers with their new AT-3 Sagger anti-tank rockets. Overhead, American AC-130 gunships unleashed a deadly stream of 20-mm rounds against the attackers, while U.S. jets bombed tanks and attempted to silence the enemy artillery. Small groups of ARVN soldiers fought desperately to defend their positions, but there was no coordinated resistance and the complete collapse of command leadership signaled the end for the 42d ARVN Regiment. It was every man for himself, as the survivors attempted to break out and flee toward Kontum. By the next day the North Vietnamese were in complete control of Tan Canh.

A similar fate befell Dak To II, just five miles to the west, following an unsuccessful attempt on April 23 by armored cavalry troops and supporting infantry from Ben Het to reinforce the garrison. The relief column was caught in an ambush as it made its way along Route 512 and was completely wiped out, losing all its equipment in the process. With their last hope of reinforcements gone, any resistance by the understrength 47th ARVN Regiment collapsed and the base fell to the North Vietnamese. Over the

ARVN troops look on as friendly aircraft unleash their payloads on the advancing enemy west of Dong Ha, April 1972.

course of the next several days, the North Vietnamese consolidated their grip over the area and their control over Route 14 east of Rocket Ridge by seizing Dien Binh after overpowering two battalions of Regional Force (RF) militia. Meanwhile, American aircraft were busy destroying the large stockpiles of ammunition and equipment left behind before they fell into communist hands.

The introduction of the man-portable, shoulder-fired SA-7 surface-to-air missiles posed a new and serious threat to low-flying American and South Vietnamese aircraft. (Photo National Museum of the U.S. Air Force)

The road to Kontum was now wide open, but the North Vietnamese tarried, failing to exploit their success and push forward. It is unclear why, but their official history cites a lack of prepositioned supplies, difficult road travel, and the need to bring additional heavy equipment forward,[24] although a rigid operational doctrine and lack of battlefield initiative are also likely to blame. Nonetheless, "it was the dumbest possible thing they could have done," recalled one U.S. adviser, "and I'm very grateful they did because there was nobody to stop them except a few people like me with pistols."[25] Indeed, with the disintegration of the 22d Division and its sister regiments of the 23d ARVN Division scattered across the southern half of the Central Highlands, there was little to stop the enemy advance. General Dzu finally collapsed under the strain and begged to be relieved, so John Paul Vann "gave up all pretense of South Vietnamese command, took over himself, and openly issued orders."[26] One of his first actions was to place the responsibility for the defense of Kontum with Colonel Ly Tong Ba, the 23d ARVN Division commander. Few thought the city could hold out given what had transpired over the past two weeks, but Vann had different ideas.

The American Response

The timing of the North Vietnamese offensive not only caught the Americans off guard, but they were also not prepared for its size, intensity, and scope that threatened to completely upend the peace negotiations. While Nixon's phased troop withdrawal from Vietnam was politically calculated to undercut his most vehement anti-war critics and allow time for Vietnamization to take hold, it also inevitably put Washington in a highly vulnerable position—one where the United States could be militarily too weak to respond effectively to North Vietnamese provocations, undermining its negotiating strategy. The launching of the Easter Offensive seemed to confirm this worse fear: in early May Le Duc Tho refused to discuss a ceasefire, saying to Kissinger that "the prospects for the North Vietnamese were looking good,"[27] given the situation on the ground in South Vietnam. And although the Nixon administration had few cards to play, the main one available—American air power—would prove to be ideally suited to the task at hand. Moreover, Le Duan and his politburo allies terribly misread Nixon, who was willing to push the limits of military brinksmanship to ensure his legacy of bringing America peace with honor in Vietnam. If the North Vietnamese wanted a fight, then by God they were going to get one. Or as Nixon bluntly put it, "The bastards have never been bombed like they're going to be bombed this time."[28]

At the start of 1972 the United States still maintained a formidable force of 385 aircraft (less than one-third strike) in South Vietnam and another 448 (nearly half of them strike) at bases in Thailand,[29] while Navy aircraft carriers operating in the Gulf of Tonkin added an additional 200 aircraft to the total.[30] It would be these air assets that would be called upon to deliver Washington's initial response to the North's invasion. The most pressing need, however, was to bring overwhelming force to bear as quickly as possible and this required massive aerial reinforcements.

The first U.S. aircraft reinforcements to arrive in early April were Marine and Air Force F-4 Phantoms out of Japan and Korea, but the majority of additional planes would

Unaccustomed to facing enemy tanks in combat, many ARVN units panicked and fled in the face of North Vietnamese armored assaults.

come directly from U.S. Air Force bases in the United States under Operation Constant Guard that began on April 11. In less than five days three Air Force Phantom squadrons along with all their men and equipment were able to deploy from the United States to Thailand and were soon flying combat missions. Another 108 F-4s, two squadrons of C-130 transports, 16 KC-135 tankers, and nearly 100 additional B-52 heavy bombers would also soon arrive in theater.[31] In all the Air Force would send the equivalent of 15 squadrons and 70,000 men to Southeast Asia in the opening months of the Easter Offensive, while the Navy would increase its air order of battle to an unprecedented six carrier air wings with more than 500 aircraft by May.[32] In short order, the number of available American strike aircraft had more than doubled. Nixon was preparing to deliver on his promise.

Although bad weather and confusion on the ground severely hampered air operations across the South in the early days of the offensive and allowed Hanoi's troops to press home their attacks and seize large chucks of territory, the improving weather, stabilizing battle lines, and freshly arriving air assets would soon allow the Americans to unleash an unparalleled torrent of aerial destruction upon the North Vietnamese—both on the southern battlefield and north of the DMZ.

Clearly, the opening round of Hanoi's offensive had dealt the South Vietnamese military a staggering blow in terms of lost men and equipment, which pushed Saigon's

South Vietnamese Rangers under enemy fire assist a wounded comrade to safety.

forces to the brink of psychological and physical collapse. Troops at An Loc were under siege and fighting for their lives. Likewise, Quang Tri and Kontum were on the verge of being cut off and encircled as the enemy closed in. In the midst of this battlefield crisis, however, U.S. advisers saw a golden opportunity, but if—and it was a big if—the defenders didn't panic. An extremely confident General James Hollingsworth reflected the attitude of senior American advisers; "Hold them [the enemy] and I'll kill them with airpower. Give me something to bomb and I'll win."[33]

And bomb them they did. At An Loc. At Quang Tri. At Kontum. A steady stream of American and South Vietnamese aircraft took to the skies to provide close air support to the embattled defenders. Forward air controllers darted in and out over the battlefields to direct strike after strike of American F-4 Phantom jets, along with VNAF A-1 Skyraiders and A-37 Dragonflies to relentlessly pound attacking NVA infantry battalions with rockets, napalm, cluster munitions, and high-explosive 500-pound bombs. U.S. Army helicopter gunships and circling Air Force AC-130 gunships also added to the carnage in the attempt to stymie the communist advance.

Most devastating of all, however, were the repeated B-52 bomber Arc Light strikes—nearly tripling to 2,000 in May—that laid waste to predetermined target boxes outside the cities.

A three-plane bomber formation could lay waste to a 1.5-mile-by-.5-mile target area with up to 90 tons of bombs that often came within a quarter mile of friendly positions, rattling the defenders and shaking the ground. As John Paul Vann noted during the defense of Kontum, "the success of many of these strikes is unquestioned" and "any time

An American F-4 Phantom provides close air support to embattled South Vietnamese troops in Quang Tri Province.

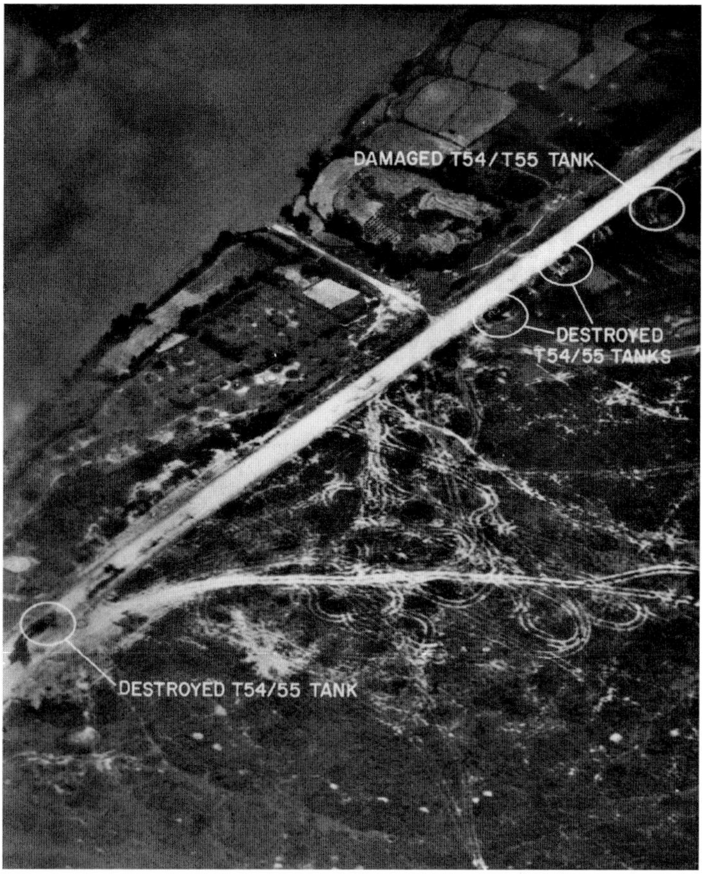

Destroyed and damaged North Vietnamese T-54/55 tanks on the road near Dong Ha in the aftermath of air strikes by VNAF A-1 Skyraiders, April 12, 1972. (Photo Naval History and Historical Command)

the wind is blowing from the north [the scene of massed Arc Light strikes] you can tell from the battlefield stench that the strikes are effective."[34] Le Duan had decided to fight a conventional war in the hope of vanquishing the South Vietnamese military and causing the collapse of the Thieu government, but now he was paying a steep price. Whole NVA units were being wiped out or rendered combat ineffective. No rear areas were safe from this American aerial assault and, most important of all, Hanoi's exposed northern supply lines came under attack too.

For the first time since the end of the Rolling Thunder bombing campaign in November 1968, targets in North Vietnam became fair game for American aircraft as Operation Freedom Train got underway on April 6. This new air campaign targeted Hanoi's extended supply lines, lines of communication, logistics facilities, and supporting military infrastructure from the DMZ northward to the 20th parallel, to impede the vital southern flow of reinforcements, equipment, and supplies needed to maintain the momentum of the Nguyen Hue Campaign. While support to the South Vietnamese ground troops was still the number one air priority, the newly appointed Seventh Air Force commander, General John Vogt, dedicated considerable assets to the new air campaign against the North.

The Indispensable Man: John Paul Vann

John Paul Vann, America's "indispensable man" in Military Region 2. (Photo U.S. Agency for International Development)

On the night of June 9, 1972 one of the most respected and experienced Americans in Vietnam—John Paul Vann—met his death in a helicopter crash on the cusp of his most significant accomplishment: the defense of Kontum city and the repulse of the North Vietnamese invasion of the Central Highlands.

A Korean War veteran, a U.S. Army Ranger, and outspoken critic of U.S. policy as an American military adviser to the South Vietnamese army in the early 1960s, Vann saw political reform and accountability as the way forward for a democratic, anti-communist South Vietnam. He resigned his commission in protest over U.S. support to the highly corrupt Ngo Dinh Diem government in 1963, but soon returned to Vietnam to work as a civilian representative of the U.S. Agency for International Development (USAID) in its rural pacification program. Vann gained a reputation for his bravery—if not recklessness—as well as for his fierce independence and unrelenting demands for political and economic reforms in his efforts to win the hearts and minds of rural Vietnamese. Always outspoken in his views, his success in the southern regions of the country propelled him quickly upwards through the senior ranks of USAID in Vietnam.

Following the 1968 Tet Offensive, which Vann saw as changing a civil war into an outright invasion by the North, he became a strong advocate of Vietnamization and of building the South Vietnamese military into a conventional fighting force capable of standing on its own. In his mind, the only way to counter North Vietnamese aggression was through the use of overwhelming firepower. Although he had once expressed gritty admiration for the Viet Cong in fighting for their cause, he despised the North Vietnamese as would-be invaders seeking to impose their will over the South.

In May 1971, he was named senior U.S. adviser to II Corps, normally a billet reserved for a two-star general, as an official endorsement of his standing and of his personal drive and dedication to the South Vietnamese cause. Full of energy, often impatient and domineering, and always leading by example, "Vann seemed at time to hold II Corps together by the very strength of his will," according to one American observer. This in turn won him the respect, confidence, and admiration of the South Vietnamese that he worked with and he was able to make demands that would have been resented by any other American adviser.

Vann's leadership would be sorely tested with the North Vietnamese thrust into II Corps' area of responsibility in April 1972, but he would be up to the task. In the opening weeks of the campaign as Lieutenant General Ngo Dzu broke down under the strain of command, Vann became the quintessential military commander. Nearly always at the center of the action, he piloted his own helicopter behind enemy lines to aid isolated U.S. advisers, barked encouragement to wavering ARVN commanders, and helped coordinate badly needed air strikes. He personally took charge in organizing the defense of Kontum around the 23d ARVN Division and his protégé, Colonel Ly Tong Ba, was well rewarded in repelling repeated North Vietnamese assaults on the city. The battle for Kontum would be the high watermark and the turning point of the enemy campaign in the Central Highlands. Lieutenant General William McCaffrey was so impressed by Vann's valor and accomplishments that he wrote him saying that "few soldiers in our history have had to cope with the challenges you face. I have never known anyone so uniquely qualified by courage, energy, and the ability to do a tough job. From where I sit, John Paul, you are a blooming hero."

While most American advisers—even highly experienced ones—could be easily replaced, the same was not true for Vann. "John is too good," recalled a friend of his, and "when he finally gets killed, and he will be one of these days, I shudder to think what will happen to the people he's been advising. He has become closer to being the indispensable man than any other in Vietnam, and that's a very dangerous thing." Vann would die likely knowing that he had helped turn the tide of battle, but fortunately he would not live to see the end of his dream of an independent, anti-communist South Vietnam when Saigon fell to the North Vietnamese three years later.

Adapted from D. Fulghum and T. Maitland, *South Vietnam on Trial*, p. 157;
L. Sorley, *A Better War*, p. 344.

The first Freedom Train strikes focused on attacking key logistics and transportation centers at Vinh and Dong Hoi, as well as against rail and road traffic along Highway 1. This would not be an easy task given the time Hanoi had to prepare and its greatly augmented air defenses throughout the southern panhandle. But the Americans had upped their game too. On April 9, a formation of 12 B-52s supported by dozens of Air Force and Navy aircraft struck the railyard and an underground petroleum, oil, and lubricants (POL) storage facility at Vinh in the first use of the heavy bombers over North Vietnam since October 1968.[35] Following up this attack three days later, 18 B-52s out of U-Tapao air base, Thailand, struck the MiG airfield at Bai Thuong, about 25 miles west northwest of Thanh Hoa. On April

American advisers stood shoulder-to-shoulder with their South Vietnamese counterparts on the front lines, despite having no official ground combat role. Several dozen would be killed, wounded or captured during the fighting.

21 and 23, more bomber missions were launched against warehouse complexes near Thanh Hoa that involved 36 U-Tapao-based bombers; one bomber was heavily damaged by an SA-2 missile during the April 23 attack and forced to divert to Da Nang for an emergency landing.[36] Before the end of the month American pilots achieved a major psychological victory too. On April 27 Air Force F-4s from the 8th Tactical Fighter Wing (TFW) out of Ubon air base, Thailand, used five 2,000-pound electro-optically guided bombs to collapse part of the western span of the Thanh Hoa bridge—the infamous Dragon's Jaw bridge that had defied Rolling Thunder attacks for more than three years—and close it to traffic.[37]

To remove any doubt that Washington was prepared to escalate its air campaign further if the North continued its attacks in the South, President Nixon approved a limited one-day attack— Operation Freedom Porch Bravo—against key logistics targets in the Haiphong and Hanoi complexes in the pre-dawn hours of April 16. Seventeen U-Tapao-based B-52s unloaded 460 tons of bombs on Haiphong's main POL storage facility, igniting intense fires and triggering secondary explosions. A post-strike damage photo assessment indicated that 17 POL storage tanks, along with several nearby warehouses, railroad tracks, and 30 pieces of rolling stock had been destroyed in the attack.[38] A second and third wave of close to 100 American aircraft soon followed with strikes by Air Force F-4s on Hanoi's main POL storage facility and by Navy A-7 Corsairs against Haiphong's Cat Bi and Kien An airfields and on several warehouse and storage complexes in the Haiphong area. As Nixon quipped after the raids, "we really left them our calling card this weekend."[39]

Nonetheless, neither the attacks on Haiphong and Hanoi nor the ongoing Freedom Train operations south of the 20th parallel did little to change the minds of the North Vietnamese leadership in light of their successes on the South Vietnamese battlefield. With Hanoi feeling its oats and General Abrams reporting from Saigon that "it is quite possible that the South Vietnamese have lost the will to fight,"[40] Nixon had little choice but to up the ante and unleash the full might of American air power against the North. Escalating the war at this point was a huge political and military gamble, but one Nixon felt he had little choice. The war needed to be settled and if Hanoi wouldn't do that in Paris, then Washington would try to do it on the battlefield.

Above: Hundreds of American and South Vietnamese forward air controllers worked hand in hand to coordinate and direct desperately needed air strikes. (Photo National Museum of the U.S. Air Force)

Below: With bad weather often obscuring the battlefield in the opening weeks of the campaign, U.S. Navy ships would provide essential fire support to government forces in Quang Tri Province. (Photo U.S. Navy)

3. TEETERING ON THE BRINK

Less than a month into Hanoi's offensive and despite massive doses of American airpower, the situation on the ground was growing increasingly desperate for Saigon's forces on all three fronts. Three ARVN divisions had lost more than half their combat strength and their remnants were barely hanging on to their positions. Dozens of artillery pieces and hundreds of tanks, armored personnel carriers, and trucks had been abandoned, destroyed, or captured by the enemy. The country's strategic reserves of Airborne and Marine brigades had been committed to plug the breaches, but fighting had taken a heavy toll on these units as well. There was very little fight left in some units as morale sank. Frontline commanders tried desperately to shore up their defensive lines amid the realization that no reinforcements were in the offing, as they prayed for fair weather and salvation from the skies above in the form of American and South Vietnamese air strikes. But would it be enough?

The Fall of Quang Tri and the Defense of Hue

After regrouping and resupplying their forces, the North Vietnamese began a broad assault on April 27 against General Giai's improvised western defenses that were manned by a hastily stitched together collection of ARVN soldiers, Rangers, and Marines. At about the same time, elements of 304th NVA Division began an aggressive push toward the coast to interdict Highway 1 just north of the O'Khe River and fire support base Nancy, which lay just north of the border with Thua Thien Province. Rumors of an enemy breakthrough west of Quang Tri soon reached General Lam at I Corps headquarters in Hue, causing him to order his pet unit, the 20th Tanks, out of the line west of Dong Ha to deal with the reported threat. While there was no threat to address, the sudden withdrawal of the armor in the Dong Ha area not only left a major gap in the defenses, but sowed panic among the infantry. Units began withdrawing on their own volition and any remaining semblance of military cohesion among the remnants of the 3d Division collapsed; the 57th ARVN Regiment became combat-ineffective. Isolated pockets of resistance were soon forced to abandon their positions in the face of building enemy pressure and a general retreat soon gave way to a headlong dash toward the Thach Han River and Quang Tri city.

General Giai's attempt to halt the rush southward and reconstitute a new defensive position around the Ai Tu combat base just north of the Thach Han River on April 30 fell victim to the growing chaos. Conflicting higher command orders, ammunition and fuel shortages, and the wounding and evacuation of the 1st Armored Brigade commander ended all hope of making a defensive stand outside Quang Tri. American and VNAF aircraft continued to strike attacking columns, but they could do only so much given the anarchy on the ground. Orders from General Lam on April 30 to "hold at all costs" only further compounded the confusion and were impossible to enforce anyway as soldiers in droves abandoned their weapons, stripped off their uniforms, and joined the hordes of civilians fleeing southward along Highway 1. The rout was on.

A few units like the 147th Marine Brigade and elements of the 20th Tanks tried to fight a rearguard action to delay the enemy's advance, but the situation was hopeless. Moreover, they would soon find themselves cut off and forced to fight their way south across the Thach Han River as best as possible. Likewise, Giai's planned defensive stand in Quang Tri itself failed to materialize as enemy artillery rained thousands of shells down on the city. A handful of Marines and Rangers, plus a few armored vehicles, could do little to mount any effective resistance. The city would soon fall to the enemy, on May 2, the first provincial capital to be captured since 1968. By early May the entirety of Quang Tri Province would be in communist hands as the North Vietnamese troops set their sights on Hue.

AH-1 Cobra attack helicopters with their 20-mm mini-guns and rockets helped turn the tide during the battles for An Loc and Kontum.

Meanwhile, the fleeing mass of humanity continued to clog the road south of Quang Tri heading toward the My Chanh River and the old imperial city of Hue. As this exodus gained a feverish momentum, military equipment was abandoned wholesale, cars and buses jammed the road, vehicles broke down or ran out of gas, and refugees mixed in with the fleeing soldiers as they all struggled to make their way toward the safety of Hue, 35 miles to the south. The roadway, however, soon became an indiscriminate killing zone as the fleeing columns were forced to run a gauntlet of 130-mm artillery fire and automatic weapons fire from North Vietnamese ambushes along what would later come to be known as "Terror Boulevard." The carnage was so great that even months later the smell of death and destruction would still linger, with "many wrecked vehicles containing a grisly cargo of corpses, shriveled, blackened mummies"[1] amid the debris of war that stretched for miles. There was never a reliable count of the dead, though it surely numbered into the thousands.[2]

On the other hand, there was a clear accounting of the devastating losses in men and matériel suffered by I Corps during the April fighting: the 3d ARVN Division had become "totally ineffective as a unit and could not be rebuilt merely by furnishing personnel and equipment." The Marines suffered some 1,000 casualties, and more than 1,500 Rangers

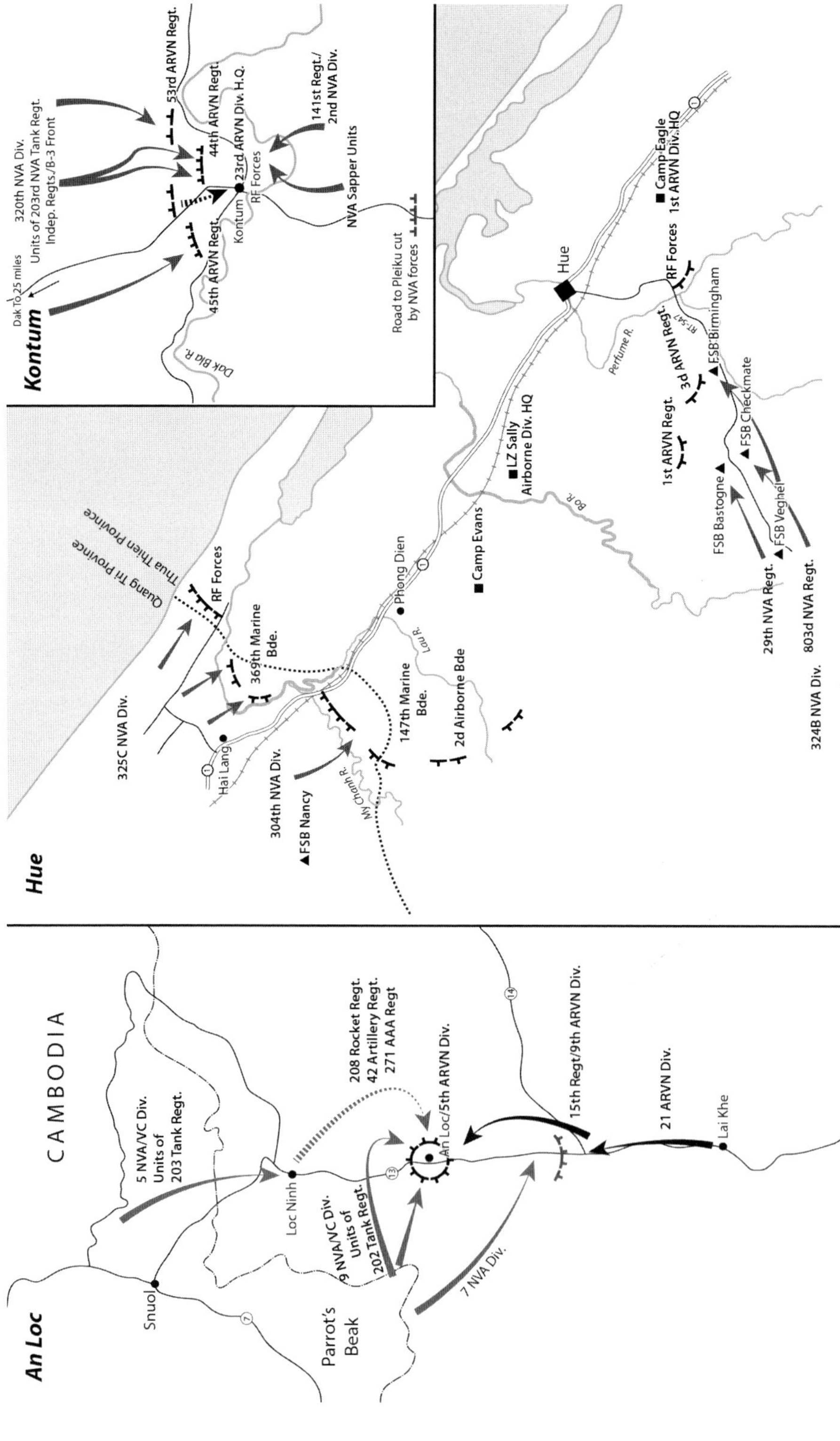

Source: Q. Truong, The Easter Offensive, p. 55: D. Fulghum and T. Maitland, South Vietnam on Trial, p. 152

Map 6: The Fight for Hue, An Loc, and Kontum.

were listed as killed, wounded or captured, with one Ranger Group losing most of its officers and suffering more than 50 percent casualties.[3] The 1st Armored Brigade "was almost nonexistent" as combat losses were compounded when tanks and armored vehicles had to be abandoned or destroyed by their crews; only one M48 and six M41 tanks and a handful of armored personnel carriers from a force of three armored cavalry squadrons and one tank regiment made it across the My Chanh River. The final tally showed the brigade suffering 1,171 casualties—a nearly 60 percent casualty rate—along with the loss of more than 400 vehicles, including 43 M48 and 66 M41 tanks and over 100 armored personnel carriers.[4] Likewise, nearly all I Corps' heavy 105-mm and 155-mm howitzers north of the river were lost, either destroyed or captured on the battlefield.

The loss of Quang Tri Province and the heavy losses there led President Thieu, at the urging of General Abrams, to recall General Lam to Saigon. The politically well-connected Lam was kicked upstairs in the Ministry of Defense and replaced with General Ngo Quang Truong, the veteran and well-respected IV Corps commander. General Giai was not so fortunate. He would become the scapegoat for the debacle that befell I Corps' northern command, being tried and convicted for "dissertation [sic] in the face of the enemy."[5] Many Americans disagreed with the harsh treatment: "He did the best he could with what he had," believed Major General Frederick Kroesen, the I Corps senior U.S. adviser, while Lieutenant General William McCaffrey thought that "the 3d ARVN Division conducted itself creditably" and blamed ensuing problems on higher command levels.[6]

The extensive U.S. airlift capability allowed Saigon to rush critical reinforcements to frontlines, as well as to launch aerial assaults behind enemy lines.

There was little time for reflection, however, as the North Vietnamese advanced on Hue and Thua Thien Province in the opening week of May. Truong's appointment brightened an otherwise bleak outlook that General Kroeson saw as "grave, but not hopeless."[7] But there was much to be done. Since the beginning of the year, Hanoi had been pushing troops and supplies into the A Shau Valley in anticipation of a thrust toward Hue from the southwest by the 324B NVA Division. Aggressive operations by the 1st ARVN Division and B-52 Arc Light strikes had kept the enemy at bay and upset his preparations, but in late April Lieutenant General Tran Van Quang made his move. On April 28, as the fighting raged in Quang Tri Province, the 29th and 803d NVA regiments assaulted and successfully overran fire support base Bastogne, the strongest position on Hue's southwestern flank. With the subsequent forced evacuation of other vulnerable 1st ARVN Division outposts astride Route 547, the path to the city was now wide open.

On May 2, reinforced elements of the 324B Division continued their push toward Hue by unleashing heavy rocket and artillery fire on the 1st Division's 3d ARVN Regiment that was occupying the high ground west of the Perfume River. Meanwhile, other troops from the 304th NVA Division closed in on the My Chanh River defensive line from the north as the last remaining survivors from Quang Tri Province scampered to safety across the river. These were not the only threats to Hue, however, as thousands of rampaging South Vietnamese deserters filled the city's streets spreading fear and panic among the city's residents and frightened refugees, until General Truong issued shoot-to-kill orders to restore order.

An ARVN M107 self-propelled 175-mm howitzer fires on enemy positions north of Hue in May 1972.

Most important, the personal arrival of Truong and his forward headquarters to Hue brought an immediate boost in morale and a new aggressive attitude that bespoke confidence in his troops. Three Marine brigades—including the battered 147th Brigade—were grouped into a single divisional command, which formed an L-shaped defensive line extending from the coast along the My Chanh River before turning southeast toward the Bo River. The remainder of the defensive perimeter south of the Bo River and west of city was held 1st ARVN Division and supplemented by territorial Regional Force units. The arrival of the 2d Airborne Brigade on May 8 further strengthened the northern sector and brought Truong's troop strength up to nearly 30,000 men, but would it be enough to counter enemy thrusts from the north and southwest?

A wrecked M41 Walker Bulldog tank near Quang Tri city, April 1972. General Lam's 1st Armor Brigade would lose hundreds of tanks and armored vehicles in the first month of fighting.

General Truong, however, wasn't about to wait and see. Unlike his predecessor, he adopted an aggressive approach, whereby his commanders were given a free hand to conduct limited attacks to destroy and disrupt enemy concentrations in their sectors. He also improved and streamlined the use of employing U.S. firepower support that allowed "sustained offensive fire conducted on a large scale."[8] Known as *Loi Phong* (Thunder Hurricane), these firepower offensives—that included heavy artillery, air strikes, and naval gunfire—were intended to completely obliterate every worthwhile target detected and prevent the enemy from massing men and matériel for an assault on the city. One U.S. Marine adviser called them "the heaviest artillery barrage I have ever heard."[9]

The much-improved weather at the beginning of May also aided in Hue's defense by allowing the full might of American and South Vietnamese air power to be unleashed. Tactical air strikes repeatedly thwarted ground attacks, B-52 Arc Light strikes hammered troop concentrations, and teams of FACs and gunships hunted down elusive batteries of 130-mm artillery pieces. It wasn't a walk in the park, however, as Hanoi had moved large numbers of 37-mm and 57-mm anti-aircraft weapons and man-portable SA-7 missiles unto the northern battlefield, downing ten American aircraft in April and May.[10] At the same time, the U.S. Air Force instigated "the most intensive in-country interdiction campaign of the war," according to General Vogt. Every significant bridge north of the My Chanh River to the DMZ was put out of service. Supply convoys were caught on open roads and annihilated. And columns of tanks, armored vehicles, and artillery moving toward the front were subjected to near constant aerial attack. According to its official history, it took the 325C NVA Division 15 days after leaving the DMZ in early May to

American adviser reviewing the situation in Military Region 1 with his counterparts. In addition to helping to organize government defenses, the U.S. adviser presence provided an invaluable morale boost government troops.

reach Quang Tri city "amidst earth-shattering B-52 bomb runs and violent enemy artillery barrages" that resulted in "a significant number of casualties."[11]

To further keep the North Vietnamese off balance, Truong's Marines launched a spoiling operation on May 13 in the Hai Lang vicinity, some six miles south of Quang Tri city. Two battalions were airlifted into position by U.S. helicopters and then swept south, catching the 66th NVA Regiment by surprise. A few days later, 1st ARVN Division troops air-assaulted the enemy position at fire support base Bastogne and captured it, linking up a few days later with forces pushing southwest to recover most of the ground the division lost in late April. These operations, along with Truong's firepower offensives, not only provided a big morale boost to the defenders, but they also began to wear on the enemy with the 324B NVA Division apparently "suffering from a severe personnel shortage" by mid-May, according to U.S. intelligence.[12]

The North Vietnamese, however, weren't done yet. On May 21 they launched a three-pronged combined infantry and armored assault across the My Chanh line, thrusting south along the coastal highway. RF militia broke in the face of the attack and the momentum pushed the Marines back some three miles. Thanks however to the timely arrival of an ARVN armored cavalry unit and heavy air strikes, the invaders were forced

Soldiers of the 20th Tank Regiment ride atop a captured T-59 tank—the Chinese variant of the Soviet T-54/55—near Dong Ha, April 1972.

back across the river. The enemy attacked again the next day, leading to close combat fighting and the extensive use of the new LAW rockets to break up armored assaults. Following two days of intense fighting the enemy had little to show for its efforts, leaving behind 542 dead and at least ten tanks and armored personnel carriers destroyed.[13] A few days later, troops from the 324B Division's 88th NVA Regiment, supported by T-54/55 and PT-76 tanks, struck the far western flank of the Marine line, but were also repulsed with heavy losses.

By the end of May the worst had apparently passed for the embattled troops of I Corps as enemy attacks sputtered to an end. During a surprise visit on May 28 President Thieu praised the defenders, whose stout resistance of Hue had not only saved the city, but cost the enemy nearly 3,000 dead and some 64 tanks and armored vehicles destroyed.[14] It was now time for General Truong to begin looking north across the My Chanh River toward retaking Quang Tri.

The Siege of An Loc

If the situation in the north of the country was bleak following the enemy's capture of Quang Tri in early May, it was even gloomier down in III Corps as the North Vietnamese prepared to crush the life out of the beleaguered garrison at An Loc once and for all. Following the failure of the April attempts to capture the city, the commanding officer of the 9th NVA/VC Division was replaced by the 5th NVA/VC Division commander—the victor of Loc Ninh—who vowed to take An Loc "within two days" of launching his assault.[15] To this end, he amassed the three regiments of his division, plus two regiments of the 7th NVA Division and the remnants of two battered 9th Division regiments, or roughly 20,000 men along with all available armored and heavy artillery assets in the region. Probing the ARVN defenses began on May 9, signaling that a major assault was imminent.

Hunkered down in their trenches, bunkers, and among the rubble of the city that they still controlled were some 4,000 men from Brigadier General Le Van Hung's 5th ARVN Division, the survivors of Task Force 52, the 3d Ranger Group, and an airborne Ranger battalion. Not only were his weary and hungry troops outnumbered, but the enemy's strong foothold in the northern part of the city and new incursions against the western perimeter had created a palpable fear that permeated the 5th Division headquarters as the heavy shelling began on the night of May 10. More than 8,000 artillery and mortar rounds would be unleashed against the defenders that night and into the early morning hours. "Some of Hung's people were wringing their hands and were a little distraught; they were obviously fatigued and nervous," recalled an American adviser on the eve of the attack.[16]

As the bombardment lifted, the enemy attack got underway, on May 11, with the 5th NVA/VC Division spearheading the assault with infantry and tanks from the north, while elements of the 9th NVA/VC Division struck from the west. The goal was to split the city in two, thereby shattering any remaining form of organized resistance. Despite some initial success by the northern thrust in advancing down the main avenue, fierce resistance by paratroopers rushed to the critical sector, extensive use of

The aftermath of a B-52 Arc Light strike. The Air Force would fly almost 4,500 Arc Light missions across South Vietnam in May and June alone.

M72 anti-tank weapons, and precisely coordinated close air support missions brought the advance to a halt. Now immobilized, the North Vietnamese troops in the salient were bombed relentlessly from the air, with nearly 300 tactical air sorties being flown on May 11 alone.[17] On the western perimeter the 7th ARVN Regiment, now reinforced, was able to slow the advance enough to allow VNAF Skyraiders and American AC-130 Spectre gunships to reap a deadly harvest. It was however, the arrival of the big bombers that finally broke the back of the North Vietnamese assault. Beginning at 9 a.m. and for the next 25 hours—one every 55 minutes—B-52 Arc Light strikes rained death upon enemy armor and infantry formations. Some strikes came within 600 yards of friendly positions, the shockwaves knocking the defenders off their feet and leaving their ears ringing. One such strike saved the 81st Airborne Ranger battalion from being overrun, while reportedly annihilating an entire regiment of the 5th NVA/VC Division.[18]

The fighting began to peter out later in the day with much of the city lying in ruins, its approaches a moonscape of bomb craters, smoldering wrecks of tanks—all 40 of those engaged were destroyed or disabled—and heaps of bodies as far as the eye could see. Many a defender wondered how they had survived such an inferno. In retrospect the tide

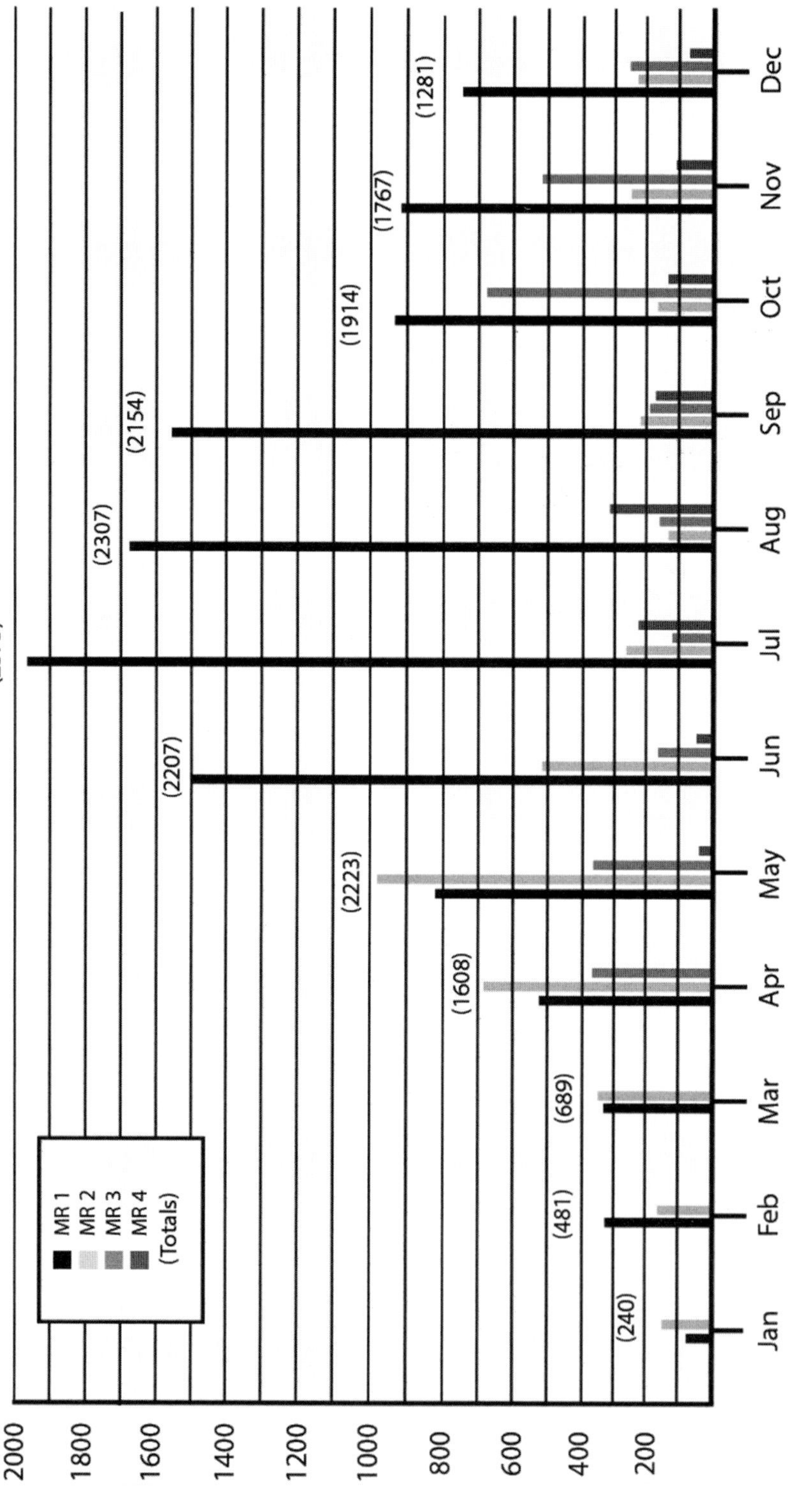

Source: E. Hartsook and S.Slade, *Air War Vietnam Plans and Operations*, p. 312.

Graph 2: B-52 Arc Light Strikes in South Vietnam

ARVN mechanized troops observe an air strike on enemy positions near An Loc in early April 1972.

had turned. Though the North Vietnamese would mount several more assaults over the next few days, they were easily blunted by a near constant steam of tactical air strikes and Arc Light missions. They were "simply trying to pile on and pile on and pile on" and "frittered away an awful lot of manpower" in futile attacks that didn't stand a chance of succeeding, according to an American adviser.[19] Licking their wounds and now short of ammunition, supplies, and equipment, the North Vietnamese now settled in to lay siege to the city, while turning their attention toward fending off Saigon's attempted relief efforts from the south.

For more than three weeks the men of the 21st ARVN Division had fought tooth and nail against two regiments of the 7th Division, to advance up Route 13 to just north of Chon Thanh. By May 13, the relief column, however, was still some 15 miles shy of An Loc. Moreover, it was facing its biggest challenge at the Tau O chokepoint; a heavily fortified and well-prepared enemy was now reinforced by the 7th Division's 209th NVA Regiment that refused to be dislodged despite massive artillery and air bombardment. Time after time the South Vietnamese attacked, but our soldiers "tenaciously held on to ... the main blocking positions while organizing mobile ones to counterattack the enemy," according to an official North Vietnamese account of the battle.[20] Try as they might, the 32nd ARVN Regiment, which had suffered some 40 percent casualties, could not make any headway and General Minh called in air support to reduce the enemy position by early June.

In the meantime, a new effort was made by III Corps to relieve the pressure on An Loc. Elements of the recently arrived 15th ARVN Regiment, 9th Division and the division's armored cavalry would swing to the east of Route 13 and Tau O to secure the village of Tan Khai, about ten miles south of An Loc. Here they could establish a fire support base to assist in the city's defense, as well as threaten the enemy blocking position at Tau O. By May 17, the South Vietnamese had secured the position and airlifted in batteries of 105-mm and 155-mm howitzers to create a formidable threat. In response, on May 20, the enemy diverted forces from An Loc to launch increasingly desperate attacks—including some in broad daylight—over the course of the next three days in an attempt to dislodge the ARVN force. Although unsuccessful in their efforts, the continuing North Vietnamese pressure did prevent Tan Khai from becoming a staging area for any future relief operations.

Nonetheless, the danger to An Loc had passed. By late May, troops of the 5th ARVN Division were once again patrolling outside the city perimeter and clearing lingering pockets of resistance. The last enemy troops were driven out of the northern and western salient by June 12. A regiment of the 18th ARVN Division was airlifted into the city a few days later and over a two-day period 1,650 fresh troops streamed into the city while more than 1,000 wounded ARVN were evacuated. Hill 169, the key high ground south of the

Following its early April encirclement, the garrison at An Loc became entirely dependent on aerial resupply. (Photo National Museum of the U.S. Air Force)

Rushing to evacuate wounded government troops from An Loc.

city that had been lost two months earlier, was recaptured on June 17, as ARVN troops went over to a generalized counterattack. A confident General Minh declared the siege officially lifted on June 18 and released the 1st Airborne Brigade even though the North Vietnamese continued to block Route 13 south of the city.

All this had come at quite a cost for both sides. More than 7,000 South Vietnamese troops had been killed or wounded and 1,000 civilians had died during the fighting with thousands more becoming refugees. The 5th ARVN Division took the brunt, suffering 30 percent casualties and, being deemed combat-ineffective, it was pulled from the line in mid-July. It was much worse for the three engaged NVA divisions—upward of 25,000 casualties, according to U.S. post-battle estimates.[21] The vast majority were caused by the devastating impact of American firepower, especially B-52 Arc Light strikes, that North Vietnamese ground commanders greatly underestimated in their approach to, and conduct of, the battle.

The Battle for Kontum

As the fighting was reaching its climax at An Loc in mid-May, the battle for Kontum in the Central Highlands was shaping up as the North Vietnamese made final preparations to seize the provincial capital and in the process break the back of II Corps. The noose around the city had been steadily tightening since the fall of Tan Canh and Dak To II. Route 14 south to Pleiku had been cut in early May and the loss of the northern and western outposts at Vo Dinh and Polei Kleng had pushed the defensive perimeter back to within eight miles of Kontum. Extensive enemy road-building was reportedly underway to speed the delivery of supplies to forward staging areas near Vo Dinh and prisoner interrogations revealed on May 10 that the 320th NVA Division was massing north of Kontum. All the warning signs were there.

Since relocating his 23d ARVN Division headquarter to Kontum in late April and taking charge of the city's defense, Colonel Ly Tong Ba had worked tirelessly to shore up his position and streamline his command by replacing the Ranger groups—at the urging of senior American adviser John Paul Vann—with his own division's regiments. Thus, the 44th ARVN and 45th ARVN regiments joined their sister regiment, the 53d ARVN Regiment, to constitute the bulk of Ba's forces. Other than a handful of RF and Popular Force (PF) territorial units to protect the city, the 23d Division would be on its own as the well of Saigon's reinforcements had long run dry with the desperate fighting around Hue and An Loc. Anticipating the enemy's major thrust from the north and northwest, Colonel Ba created a series of hardened positions arcing just north of Kontum that were anchored by the Dak Bla River on the left flank, extending across Route 14, and over to Route 58 on the right flank. These would be occupied by troops

At the urging of General Abrams, Lieutenant General Ngo Quang Truong (holding rifle) was given command of I Corps by President Thieu in early May and charged with the defense of Hue and the recapture of Quang Tri city.

ARVN soldiers carry a wounded comrade during their retreat in the Central Highlands, April 1972.

from the 23d Division. The south of the city would be safeguarded by RF and PF troops positioned in defensive works behind the Dak Bla River.

The long-awaited attack got underway in the early morning of May 14, but unlike earlier assaults in the highlands there was no massive preliminary bombardment. Still, the enemy order of battle was imposing: five infantry regiments, plus supporting tanks and sapper units, or almost 18,000 men on the move. As expected, the main thrust came down Route 14 by elements of two regiments of the 320th Division, which were supported by T-54/55 tanks from the 203d Tank Regiment. Simultaneously, ARVN positions north and northeast of the city were also hit, while to the south of Kontum, a regiment of the 2d NVA Division and sapper elements probed positions held by RF and PF troops. Intense and highly accurate 105-mm and 155-mm gunfire rained down on the force advancing down Route 14 in "the heaviest concentration of effective artillery fire put down during the Easter Offensive by any South Vietnamese unit in II Corps."[22] This and the extensive use of M72 anti-tank weapons slowed and disrupted the infantry and armored attack, presenting inviting targets for arriving swarms of American aircraft that included Huey helicopters, newly equipped with TOW anti-tank rockets.[23] Fighting continued throughout much of the day, as the city weathered periodic rounds of heavy rocket and artillery fire, without the North Vietnamese troops making much headway.

A renewed enemy effort that night to the east of Route 14, however, succeeded in punching a hole between the 44th and 53d ARVN regiments' defensive positions that was eagerly exploited with wave after wave of infantry attacks. The situation soon

Although a civilian employee of the U.S. Agency for International Develop, John Paul Vann (center) would rise to become the senior American adviser to II Corps by early 1972 and his leadership was credited with turning the tide of battle in the Central Highlands.

became critical as both ARVN units were in danger of being cut off and overrun. Taking a desperate gamble, Colonel Ba diverted two preplanned nighttime B-52 Arc Lights strikes against the growing breach, pulling his troops out of the kill zone just as the bombers made their bombing runs. The result was "like thunderbolts unleashed over the masses of enemy troops" with explosions that "rocked the small city and seemed to cave in the rib cages of ARVN troops not far away."[24] Hundreds of North Vietnamese soldiers lay dead or dying in the strike's aftermath. The first attempt to capture Kontum had failed.

Although buoyed by this victory and a visit from the new II Corps commander, Major General Nguyen Van Toan, and John Paul Vann, the South Vietnamese knew they had just narrowly avoided disaster. There were simply too few men to properly secure the extended defensive line, so Ba moved to shorten his perimeter by withdrawing closer to the city and moving the 44th Regiment into a reserve position near the hospital. Soon the enemy was back at it, regularly shelling the city and forcing the closure of the airfield. North Vietnamese sappers and infiltrators disguised as refugees also began filtering into the south of the city through the porous militia defenses and mixing with the local population. Moreover, the enemy probes by the 2d NVA Division continued to chip away at the northern defenses, creating a dangerous salient between the 45th and 53d ARVN Regiments by May 19. The commitment of Colonel Ba's reserves, including an armored cavalry squadron with M41 tanks was able to check the enemy advance, but the situation remained precarious. Over the course of the next two days the battle seesawed back and forth with the North Vietnamese gains being neutralized by ARVN counterattacks that were supported by U.S. Cobra attack helicopters and VNAF AC-47 gunships. Hourly B-52 strikes prevented the enemy from bringing up reinforcements, while orbiting FACs directed tactical air strikes at enemy tanks and artillery emplacements. By the evening of May 21, the North Vietnamese had had enough, suffering more than 1,000 casualties. Round two had gone to the defenders, but just barely.

Seeking to capitalize on the situation, General Toan mounted an effort to reopen the road from Pleiku to Kontum on May 21 by sending two Ranger groups and armored vehicles to clear the enemy blocking position at Chu Pao Pass held by the 95B NVA Regiment. Despite heavy bombing, including the use of cluster bombs, the enemy remained firmly entrenched and efforts by the Rangers were repulsed with heavy losses. Route 14 north from Pleiku would remain closed. In the meantime, Colonel Ba used the lull to probe the enemy positions to the north of the city with his men reporting massive devastation—a landscape of twisted masses of rock and shattered trees, littered with bomb craters, and decaying bodies as far as the eye could see. One captured survivor of the 48th NVA Regiment claimed most companies in his battalion had been reduced to about ten men during the weeks of B-52 strikes and much of their supplies had been destroyed en route to the front lines.[25]

North Vietnamese commanders failed to utilize their armor effectively in mass numbers, but instead frittered them away in small-scale attacks without proper infantry support.

Still the North Vietnamese were not done. But time was running out: men and supplies were dwindling and the Central Highlands monsoon rains were approaching. On the evening of May 24, the North Vietnamese unleashed one of their heaviest artillery and mortar barrages to date. This time, however, a regimental-size assault by elements of the 2d NVA Division and two sapper battalions was able to pierce the territorial militia defenses and establish a foothold in the city's southern sector. Meanwhile, North Vietnamese infantry supported by tanks struck the northern line near the airfield, as their artillery—which included captured 155-mm American howitzers—concentrated on silencing the South Vietnamese guns with highly accurate counterbattery fire. By the afternoon of May 25, nearly all the ARVN artillery had been put out of action, forcing Vann to declare a tactical emergency and calling upon General Abrams at MACV to send every available American aircraft to the defense of the city. This did the trick, ending the immediate threat to the northern perimeter, but house-to-house fighting still raged in the south of city.

The situation, however, deteriorated further over the next two days as the enemy threw everything he had left at Kontum's defenses. Attacking southeast down Route 14 once again with two regiments of infantry and the remaining tanks, while simultaneously

Three Air Force C-130s from the 374th Tactical Air Wing would be lost to enemy ground fire during resupply missions to the besieged garrison at An Loc during April and May. (Photo National Museum of the U.S. Air Force)

The arrival of A-7Ds at Korat, Thailand in September and October 1972 gave the Air Force a more capable ground attack aircraft that could reach all North Vietnamese targets without refueling. (Photo National Museum of the U.S. Air Force)

A-37A Dragonfly aircraft of the Air Force's 8th SOW out of Bien Hoa were some of the first to respond to the North's invasion of Binh Long Province. (Photo National Museum of the U.S. Air Force)

AC-119 gunships provided much of the defensive punch during battles in the Central Highlands and around An Loc. (Photo National Museum of the U.S. Air Force)

AC-130 gunships armed with 40-mm cannon and 20-mm mini-guns helped pour deadly fire down upon attacking North Vietnamese troops both day and night. (Photo National Museum of the U.S. Air Force)

An F-4D of the 435th TFS armed with a later version of Paveway laser-guided bombs than those used during operations Linebacker I and II. (Photo National Museum of the U.S. Air Force)

An abandoned North Vietnamese T-54/55 tank rest near a large bomb carter on the outskirts of An Loc. (Photo National Museum of the U.S. Air Force)

Above: Fierce enemy resistance took a heavy toll on ARVN troops attempting to advance north along Route 13 to break the siege of An Loc throughout May and June 1972.

Right: American B-52 Arc Light strikes inflicted devastating physical and psychological damage on North Vietnamese troops. (Photo National Museum of the U.S. Air Force)

An F-4J of VF-96 off the USS *Constellation* ready to engage enemy MiG fighters in the opening days of Operation Linebacker. (Photo Naval Aviation Museum)

Above: Haiphong's waterfront comes under attack by U.S. Navy aircraft, May 1972.

Left: Under Vietnamization, billions of dollars in military equipment—including brand-new M48A3 Patton tanks—were provided to the South Vietnamese military by the United States.

The seemingly ageless A-1 Skyraiders of the VNAF proved invaluable in providing desperately needed close air support in the early days of the campaign. (Photo National Museum of the U.S. Air Force)

Mobile ZSU-57 anti-aircraft guns were deployed to the South for the first time, in 1972, to counter the air threat. (Photo National Museum of the U.S. Air Force)

Right: Forward air controllers (FACs) flying small aircraft like the O-2A "Oscar Duce" did yeoman duty directing and coordinating air strikes. (Photo National Museum of the U.S. Air Force)

Below: Pleiku air base in the Central Highlands served as a key forward staging area for American and South Vietnamese aircraft. (Photo National Museum of the U.S. Air Force)

The F-105G Wild Weasel became an integral part of U.S. efforts to counter the SAM threat in the North. (Photo National Museum of the U.S. Air Force)

The Soviet-made SA-2 Guideline surface-to-air missile, known to U.S. pilots as the "flying telephone," was used with devastating effect against American aircraft attacking the North Vietnamese heartland. (Photo National Museum of the U.S. Air Force)

As part of the country's strategic reserve, South Vietnamese Rangers would find themselves being rushed from crisis to crisis.

An American adviser works with South Vietnamese troops to coordinate defensive preparations in Long Binh Province.

The USS *Coral Sea* and its Air Wing 15 were on station at the outbreak of offensive and soon found themselves in the thick of the fighting. (Photo U.S. Navy)

Right: A Navy F-4B of VF-111 delivers its deadly payload against the enemy. (Photo Naval Aviation Museum)

Below: The air base at Da Nang would serve as a critical hub for South Vietnamese A-1 Skyraider air operations in Military Region 1.

Above left: South Vietnamese pilot viewing results of his air strike. Despite its relatively small size, the VNAF carried much of the close air support burden throughout the fighting. (Photo National Museum of the U.S. Air Force)

Above right: Despite its older technology, South Vietnamese AC-47 gunships were able to play a significant role in the defense of key government positions. (Photo National Museum of the U.S. Air Force)

Below: The state-of-the-art F-111A (here armed with cluster bombs) was able to fly at high speeds just above ground level and strike unsuspecting North Vietnamese targets, earning it the nickname of "Whispering Death." (Photo National Museum of the U.S. Air Force)

Le Duan hoped to capitalize on the growing American anti-war movement to hamstring President Nixon's response to his invasion of the South in 1972.

Risky air drops of supplies and ammunition often became the only way to resupply cut-off government troops in the field. (Photo National Museum of the U.S. Air Force)

thrusting from the northeast into the center of Ba's defenses, the North Vietnamese hoped to overwhelm the defenders. The weight of this renewed assault largely succeeded in cutting off the 45th ARVN Regiment from the city, as it slammed headlong into the 44th Regiment's position and nearly overran the command post. Adding to the spectacle the main ammunition depot near the airfield was hit, exploding in a thunderclap and producing a huge orange ball of flame that lit up the morning sky. In the ensuing melee, the bravery of the South Vietnamese soldiers was sorely tested as they battled enemy tanks and wave after wave of NVA infantry at close quarters. Once again, the timely arrival of American Cobra gunships and TOW-equipped Hueys from Pleiku devastated the enemy armor, while B-52s dumped their deadly payloads on the attackers with precision. At night, orbiting U.S. Air Force AC-130 and AC-119 gunships provided defensive coverage to prevent the enemy from exploiting their gains, but still the enemy wormed its way into the weakened ARVN positions.

Facing an increasingly critical situation, Colonel Ba received reluctant permission from General Toan to shrink and tighten up his northern perimeter once again by falling back into the city itself on the afternoon of May 27. It was just in time. Before dawn the next day a heavy artillery barrage preceded an all-out ground assault on the new ARVN positions. It was do or die now for both sides. Exhausted, running low on ammunition, and with no further place to retreat, Colonel Ba rallied his men to hold the line, while Vann and his team of American advisers called in air strike after air strike over the course of the day—one every 20 minutes. Seeing the North Vietnamese attack falter, elements of the 44th and 53d regiments along with some M41 tanks from the 8th Armored Cavalry Regiment launched a series of successful counterattacks that finally pushed the enemy back following fierce hand-to-hand fighting. Even in the south of the city, the RF and PF militiamen were taking the fight to the enemy, rooting out sapper teams one by one across their sector.

By the afternoon of May 30, it was all over as reconnaissance teams reported seeing enemy troops hastily withdrawing to the northwest and isolated pockets of resistance were systematically eliminated. The surprise arrival of President Thieu and a team of

A-4 Skyhawks (pictured) and F-4 Phantoms carried the Navy's bombing load in the South, while the more advanced A-6 Intruders and A-7 Corsair IIs carried the burden in the North. (Photo National Museum of the U.S. Air Force)

Above: North Vietnamese troops steamrolled their way through much of Quang Tri Province in the opening weeks of the offensive, much to the delight of Le Duan and his politburo allies.

Right: A battle-weary ARVN soldier near Kontum, May 1972. The fighting took not only a heavy physical, but also a deep psychological toll on both sides.

South Vietnamese Territorial Forces

Growing the size and capability of Saigon's military was an essential element of Washington's Vietnamization strategy and much of this increased burden would fall on the country's territorial militia forces, which saw a swelling of their ranks to more than 550,000 men by 1971 and accounting for more than half the strength of South Vietnam's military at the time of the Easter Offensive.

Officially known as the Regional Forces (RF) and the Popular Forces (PF), South Vietnamese territorial forces operated in all the country's provinces and districts and fell under the administrative control of the Civil Operations and Revolutionary Development Support (CORDS) program rather than under the South Vietnamese military. Although their primary responsibility was to provide CORDS security for the country's pacification and development efforts, by the early 1970s they were also increasingly tasked with conducting localized offensive operations as well. To this end, major efforts were made to improve the quality of RF and PF units by upgrading their equipment and training. Old M1 carbines and surplus World War II equipment were replaced with new M16 rifles, M60 machine guns, and M79 grenade launchers; 95 percent of all units were modernized by 1971. Training was also vastly improved with all new territorial force personnel undergoing the standard 14 weeks of army basic training and RF and PF units in the field worked

Lightly armed, but brave South Vietnamese territorial militia troops often played a vital role in shoring up government defensive positions.

with American mobile advisory teams to improve their combat effectiveness. These improvements fueled a substantial increase in operations across the country by 1972, although lingering problems of poor discipline, low morale, and weak leadership still continued to plague some units.

The territorial militia forces would, however, face their sternest test with the onset of the Easter Offensive—one that they in large part would pass with flying colors. As ARVN troops collapsed under the weight of the North Vietnamese offensive in the opening weeks of the campaign, RF and PF units were increasingly called upon to help shore up government defenses. At An Loc they bravely manned bunkers and defensive positions alongside ARVN and Airborne troops. At Kontum they secured the southern perimeter of the city against repeated NVA attacks and hunted down infiltrating sappers. And in the defense of the Hue pocket, General Truong depended on them to supplement ARVN positions safeguarding the southwest approaches to the city. The lowly and lightly armed territorial troops would in fact become an essential component in the successful defense of these cities.

Even more critically, RF and PF troops often showed more aggressive grit than regular ARVN troops and were frequently praised by American advisers for their combat performance. Used to being on their own without artillery or air support, they proved to be tenacious on defense, consistently charging out of their bunkers and trenches to close with the enemy. The first T-54/55 tank kills at An Loc in fact were achieved by RF and PF soldiers using LAWs and by May they would rack up dozens of individual kills. As they were fighting on familiar terrain and near their families and homes, morale was generally good—not a single RF or PF unit imploded—despite the harsh conditions they endured. In the final analysis, when well led and supported the territorial troops proved to be every bit as effective as most ARVN troops. They would pay a steep price too with RF and PF units suffering some of the highest casualty rates among the defender of An Loc and Kontum.

Sources: S. Lipsman and E. Doyle, *Fighting for Time*, pp. 76-77 and D. Andrade, *America's Last Vietnam Battle*, p. 454.

journalists by helicopter from Pleiku later that day to congratulate the troops on their successful defense of the city and promote Ba to brigadier general provided the ultimate symbolism to a hard-won victory. Hanoi's troops had failed to take Kontum and paid a terrible price, suffering between 20,000 and 40,000 killed and perhaps the loss of a hundred tanks in the Central Highlands fighting.[26] Mopping-up operations would continue into June, but the threat to the region had passed. Sadly, John Paul Vann, the man who was a driving force behind the victory at Kontum, would not live much longer to see the final fruits of his labor. He would die in a helicopter crash on June 9 after reporting to General Abrams that the last enemy pocket of resistance in the city had been cleared.[27]

Respite

Although the Saigon regime was not out of danger yet, it had weathered more than two months of the best body blows that the North Vietnamese could deliver. Its military had cracked—and some ARVN units had indeed disintegrated—under the strain, but the bulk of it remained intact. Undeniably air power had come to the rescue to save the day in April and May—with the VNAF flying three-quarters of the tactical combat sorties[28]—but it would still take South Vietnamese troops on the ground to achieve victory on the battlefield. For now, however, Saigon was content use the brief lull to consolidate its position on the battlefield following its successful defenses of Hue, An Loc, and Kontum, as well as to rest, rebuild, and reequip its forces before embarking on the next round.

And there was a lot to be done given the battered state of the South Vietnamese military. At least three ARVN divisions were in need of rebuilding given their mauling; the 3d Division needing to be entirely reconstituted and rearmed. Likewise, many elite Marine, Ranger, and Airborne units had suffered serious casualties and required immediate replacements. Most significant in terms of South Vietnamese equipment were the heavy losses in artillery, tanks, and armored vehicles. It was estimated that more than 200 pieces of artillery had been destroyed, abandoned or captured. Fortunately, the Americans rushed to make good these losses, sending dozens of 105-mm guns to Da Nang even before the first attacks on Hue commenced. More difficult to replace immediately, however, would be the hundreds of tanks and armored personnel carriers lost in the fighting. Washington instituted Project Enhance in May 1972 to make good Saigon's equipment losses, but it would take many months to make them whole.

Hanoi was even worse off. Not only had the recent series of defeats across all three of its battlefronts upended the military component of its strategy, but the battered

Civilians flee the early April fighting along Route 13 in Binh Long Province.

The timely introduction by the Americans of new tube-launched, optically tracked, wire-guided (TOW) anti-tank weapons to South Vietnamese frontline troops helped them to effectively counter the enemy's armored assaults. (Photo U.S. Army)

North Vietnamese Army was a far cry from the defiant force that pushed brazenly down the highways of South Vietnam, driving all before them only a few months before. Tens of thousands of its best soldiers were dead and thousands more wounded. Its armored columns had been reduced to smoldering wrecks by enemy air attacks and many destroyed or abandoned tanks littered the streets of An Loc and Kontum or the approaches to Hue. The ongoing American air strikes on its rear areas and supply lines hindered reorganization and rearming efforts and contributed to growing shortages of food, ammunition, food, and medical supplies at the front.

While Hanoi's army had taken a severe beating, it was far from being defeated and its forces still occupied large portions of South Vietnam, especially in the north. The South Vietnamese had proven their ability to defend fixed positions, but now they would be tested on their ability to recapture lost territory in the face of determined resistance. There was still much more fighting to come. Moreover, Le Duan was learning the hard way that Nixon was more than willing to bring the pain of war directly to the North Vietnamese heartland.

4. AMERICA'S AERIAL COUNTEROFFENSIVE

Even as Saigon's forces were teetering on the brink of destruction in early May, the U.S. Joint Chiefs of Staff were finalizing plans to bring the full weight of American air power to Hanoi's doorstep for the first time since 1968 in retaliation for its launching of the Easter Offensive. It would be a truly massive undertaking. An air campaign—codename Operation Linebacker—would be like none other in the war, it would pull no punches and was designed to bring the North Vietnamese war machine to its knees. It was also a campaign that American air commanders had long sought and were determined to get right; they needed little encouragement to implement Nixon's directive of "bombing the bastards like they never been bombed before."

Opening Salvos

Although the United States had been conducting bombing and interdiction missions in North Vietnam up to the 20th parallel since early April, the new air campaign would be

F-4J Phantoms (foreground) and an A-7E Corsair II aboard the USS *Constellation* in the Gulf of Tonkin, May 1972. By mid-month, the Navy would increase its operating strength to six carriers with more than 500 aircraft. (Photo Naval History and Heritage Command)

a major escalation and a decidedly marked departure from the past. It would be first and foremost a military operation designed to destroy the North's war-making capacity, but one with a single, clear political objective of ending the war for the United States. There would be no White House micromanagement, no complex bombing restrictions or second guessing. In short, it was to be American air power unleashed.

Operation Linebacker got underway on May 10 with the first missions flown against targets in the Hanoi-Haiphong heartland, on a day that would witness some of the most intense aerial combat of the entire Vietnam War. The USS *Constellation*'s air wing began the campaign when its A-6 Intruders and A-7 Corsairs struck Haiphong's main POL storage facility. The strike was preceded by F-4 Phantom flak suppressors and A-7 Iron Hands—surface-to-air missile (SAM) suppression missions—engaging the deadly SA-2 missile batteries surrounding the city. Two more waves of some 60 Navy aircraft then joined the attack later on, cratering Haiphong's main railyard and dropping a span of the main road and rail bridge out of the city. In all, the Navy would fly nearly 300 sorties from three carriers that first day of Linebacker without the loss of a single strike aircraft.[1]

Meanwhile in the skies over Hanoi some 55 miles to the west, the Air Force was sending more than 100 attack and support aircraft into the fray. The main strike force

The USS *Hancock* would conduct its seventh war deployment during the Easter Offensive with the venerable A-4 Skyhawk providing critical air support to embattled South Vietnamese ground forces. (Photo Naval Aviation Museum)

was composed of 32 F-4s from the 8th TFW carrying an array of precision-guided and conventional munitions, while 12 F-105G Wild Weasels provided air defense suppression and 28 Phantom fighters from the 432nd TFW out of Udorn, Thailand flew air cover for the strike force.[2] In what would become a familiar routine, dozens of supporting aircraft accompanied the strike force, providing electronic countermeasures, communications, early warning, reconnaissance, rescue, and refueling. The 8th TFW's targets on the opening day were the Paul Doumer Bridge over the Red River and the railyard at Yen Vien, just to the east and northeast respectively of downtown Hanoi. As one of the best-defended cities in the world, the American pilots would be flying into the belly of the beast.

Preceding the Air Force strike groups were F-4s releasing chaff along the flight path to confuse enemy radars, while other Phantoms from the 432rd TRW flew combat air patrol to counter any Vietnamese People's Air Force (VPAF) reaction. In addition to these aircraft, each incoming strike group was accompanied by four F-105G Wild Weasels for SAM and flak suppression and four F-4 fighters providing strike escort duties.[3] Anticipation weighed heavily on the pilots and crews, who were expecting a tough fight on their return to Hanoi after a nearly four-year hiatus. And they were not disappointed. Soon the sky lit up with streams of anti-aircraft fire and the telltale smoke trails of SA-2 missiles; by mid-morning the fighter escorts found themselves engaging at least six enemy MiGs in a dogfight northwest of Hanoi. Initially the Americans got the better of the fight, downing three MiG-21 fighters with Sparrow air-to-air missiles,[4] but then a pair of MiG-19s from the 925th Fighter Regiment jumped the Americans, downing a Phantom in a hail of 30-mm fire.

In the meantime, the Paul Doumer strike force pressed on, evading barrages of anti-aircraft fire and SA-2 missiles—part of around 100 fired that day—as they approached the mile-long rail and highway bridge. All 16 of the strike F-4s were able to release their payloads on target: the four 2,000-pound electro-optically guided bombs missing, but the dozen laser-guided bombs scoring hits that severely damaged the bridge.[5] The next day the Seventh Air Force commander, General John Vogt, sent a single flight of four Phantoms armed with 2,000- and 3,000-pound laser-guided bombs to finish the job, successfully dropping three spans of the bridge and rendering it inoperable until the end of the war.[6] The other target that morning would be the nearby railyard at Yen Vien, an important transportation and logistics hub for supplies arriving from China. Sixteen Phantoms from the 8th TFW armed with conventional 500-pound bombs were given that assignment.[7] Hot on the heels of the Paul Doumer strike group, the second group of 16 F-4s and their escorts pressed northward to attack and successfully crater the main railyard at Yen Vien with 36 tons of bombs.

The day was far from over however. In the early afternoon, 90 Navy aircraft launched a major attack against the strategic town of Hai Duong that lay midway between Haiphong and Hanoi. It was home to a major railyard, a vital rail and highway bridge crossing, and a POL storage facility. Several flights of A-7 Iron Hands struck nearby SAM sites, as three waves of Corsairs and Intruders unleashed a torrent of bombs on the targets. Rising to contest the attackers were nearly two dozen VPAF MiGs in what became the

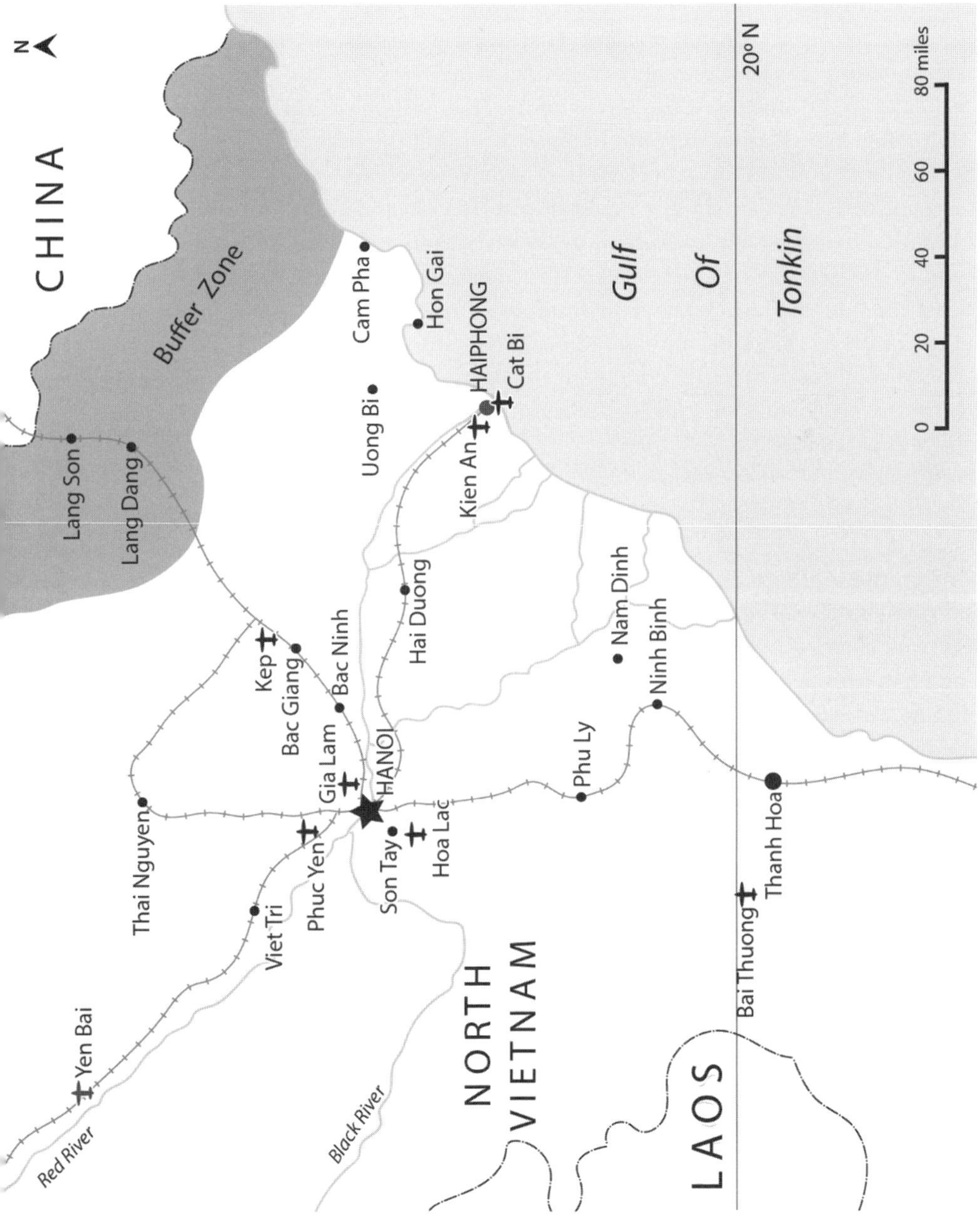

Map 7: The North Vietnamese Heartland.

largest aerial battle of the war, involving no less than 45 American and North Vietnamese aircraft. When it was all over, seven MiG-17s would be brought down by American air-to-air missiles without the loss of a single Navy fighter in aerial combat. Notably, Lieutenant Randall Cunningham and his radar intercept officer Lieutenant (j.g.) William Driscoll would rack up three kills that day in their F-4, pushing their total to five enemy aircraft and thus become the first aces of the Vietnam War.

Still later in the afternoon, the Navy bombed the harbor facilities at Hon Gai northeast of Haiphong, as well as the rail and highway bridge at the port of Cam Pha farther to the east. The most noteworthy aspect of these strikes were two wayward 500-pound bombs hitting and seriously damaging a Soviet ship at Hon Gai and killing one of the ship's crew.[8] All planes returned safely to their ships by early evening. These final missions brought an end to the first day of Linebacker with American pilots flying more than 400 sorties against the North Vietnamese heartland, leaving in their wake destroyed or heavily bridges, cratered railyards, and smoldering POL storage facilities. Eleven enemy MiGs had been shot down in aerial combat at the cost of two Air Force F-4s; two other Navy Phantoms were lost to SA-2 and anti-aircraft fire and a third was so severely damaged that it was written off.[9]

Building on the momentum of earlier Freedom Train interdiction operations in the southern panhandle, the new air campaign sought to systematically destroy the North's transportation network north of the 20th parallel and its ability to support military operations on the southern battlefield by prioritizing major bridges, key rail line segments, and logistics hubs serving as conduits for military equipment and supplies flowing southward from Hanoi and Haiphong, as well as key chokepoints along the rail and road links bringing in supplies from China.

Taking care of some old business too, Air Force pilots returned on May 13 to finish off the infamous Dragon's Jaw bridge at Thanh Hoa that had been knocked out of service in late April. This time F-4s from the 8th TFW armed with laser-guided and conventional bombs unleashed almost 69 tons of ordnance on the bridge that sent the entire western span into the Song Ma River.[10] Periodic attacks throughout the remainder of the year by the Air Force and Navy prevented its repair and kept the bridge out of service until the end of the war. Likewise, several more key rail and highway bridges along Highway 1 from Vinh southward were also knocked out by Navy strikes in the opening weeks of the campaign, thus slowing the southward flow of supplies. Meanwhile, in the far north, Air Force laser-guided bombs put out of service 13 important rail bridges along the northeast and northwest rail corridors that linked Hanoi to the Chinese border.[11] Importantly, several of these bridges were located inside the U.S. self-imposed 30 nautical mile Chinese buffer zone and were struck for the first time in the war. For example, on May 25, 20 F-4s from the 8th TFW bombed the key Lan Giai bridge only 12 miles from the Chinese border, successfully dropping six of its eleven spans, using 2,000- and 3,000-pound laser- and electro-optically guided bombs.[12] Navy Intruders and Corsairs were also able to disable four other rail bridges between Haiphong and Hanoi during the month as well.

So far Linebacker was off to a good start for the Americans with the Air Force and Navy flying over 6,000 sorties in May. Many of the key transportation targets had been

May 10, 1972 saw the opening day of Operation Linebacker, the unprecedented American air campaign against North Vietnamese transportation, economic, and military infrastructure. (Photo U.S. Navy)

successfully struck; new countermeasures, precision-guided munitions, and improved American tactics appeared to be working well; 27 VPAF MiGs had been shot down in combat; and the strategic interdiction effort was apparently beginning to have an impact as there were growing reports of ammunition, fuel, and supply shortages on the southern battlefield. This did, however, come at a cost: 20 U.S. aircraft (eleven Navy and nine Air Force) were lost, nine pilots and crewmen killed, and another 12 captured.[13]

Defending the Heartland

While undoubtedly pleased with the initial results of the air campaign, the Americans were well aware of the challenge facing them. Hanoi was more than ready to put up a fight when the Americans came calling, having spent three and half years to expand and upgrade its air defense network. By concentrating its defense resources in the critical Hanoi-Haiphong area, the North Vietnamese were able to husband their best MiG fighter regiments and layer their anti-aircraft and missile defense network to create a deadly killing zone, a zone that the American pilots would be forced to fly into to reach their targets.

Previously, the centerpiece of the North Vietnamese air defenses was the anti-aircraft gun. The more guns the better. Nearly anything that could fire was pressed into service and by the end of the 1966 it was estimated there were upward of 7,000 weapons from 12.7 mm to 85 mm deployed in an air defense role. Not surprisingly, this curtain of anti-aircraft fire took a deadly toll on the attackers, accounting for approximately two-thirds of all American aircraft losses from 1965 to 1968.[14] By the spring of 1972, however, U.S. intelligence estimated that the North's anti-aircraft weapon arsenal had declined to about 4,000 guns and fewer than 1,000 of these were 37 mm or greater.[15] Despite this overall reduction, the most important targets in the Hanoi-Haiphong region remained heavily protected by multiple anti-aircraft positions that posed a serious danger to dive-bombing aircraft.

It was, however, the expansion of the North Vietnamese surface-to-air missile coverage to the entire country by 1972 that appeared to present the greatest threat environment to American aircraft. SA-2 missiles even posed a danger to U.S. and South Vietnamese planes operating south of the DMZ during the Easter Offensive; an Air Force EB-66 electronic countermeasures aircraft supporting B-52 strikes fell victim on April 2.[16] Still, the bulk of Hanoi's missile defense was concentrated around the capital region, with ten missile battalions defending Hanoi and four more battalions protecting Haiphong.[17] It was believed that the North Vietnamese could field "perhaps 240 SA-2 launchers" rotating across some 300 pre-prepared sites; post-war analysis indicated that the actual inventory of SA-2 missiles in the spring of 1972 was likely in excess of 4,000.[18]

Better training, growing familiarization, and improved equipment also increased the potential lethality of the North's missile defenses. New tactics employing decoy sites to mimic the electronic signal of the Fan Song acquisition radars were used to confuse American pilots or force Iron Hand aircraft to waste their anti-radar homing missiles on dummy targets. Likewise, the new capability to optically fire and track SA-2 missiles negated the telltale electronic pre-launch signature, giving U.S. aircraft less warning. An improved SA-2 beacon transmitter was also adopted, which was more difficult for American electronic countermeasure equipment to jam than the older system. In addition, North Vietnamese air defense controllers often attempted to coordinate barrage firings of unguided SA-2s with attacking MiG fighters. The goal of the missile barrage was to distract and harass the American planes into evasive action and thereby allow arriving MiGs to gain a favorable attacking position. The tactic was first used successfully on May 11 to down an F-105G Wild Weasel southwest of Hanoi by MiG-21s.[19]

The third leg of the North's air defense triad tasked with defending the country's heartland was a vastly enlarged and modernized Vietnamese People's Air Force, which now numbered some 250 fighter aircraft, including 93 advanced MiG-21s with Atoll air-to-air missiles and 33 highly maneuverable Chinese-made MiG-19s armed with three 30-mm cannons.[20] Moreover, Hanoi concentrated its four main fighter regiments at bases to the northeast and northwest of the capital: the majority of the MiG-21s at Phuc Yen, MiG-19s at Yen Bai and Phuc Yen, and Kep served as the primary base for MiG-17s. Accordingly, these airfields would be subject to intense and regular American air strikes, but none of them was ever put out of service for any length of time.

Although still far outnumbered by the Americans, the North Vietnamese made the most of their fighter order of battle by taking advantage of their efficient early warning radar and ground control network, exploiting the often predictable U.S. tactics, and then using the MiG's superior close-quarters maneuvering to launch well-timed hit-and-run attacks against American strike formations and their supporting aircraft. Ground controllers typically sought to position MiG-21s above and behind enemy aircraft to enable them to make a high-speed approach from the rear to launch their Atoll missiles. Meanwhile, the more maneuverable MiG-17s and MiG-19 were positioned to make frontal high-speed passes into the enemy formations from below. In addition, North Vietnamese pilots often played a cat-and-mouse game with their American counterparts in an attempt to lure them into a MiG or anti-aircraft gun ambush. Despite the disastrous opening day of the campaign, especially for the MiG-17s of the 923rd Fighter Regiment, these fighter tactics proved highly effective early on and by the end of June VPAF pilots had achieved an unprecedented 12:13 loss ratio against their U.S. Air Force counterparts; the first time the Air Force had been on the losing end of an air-to-air ratio.[21] This was all the more galling given the Navy's 19 victories without a loss over the same period.

This changing face of North Vietnamese air defense forced American commanders to adapt as the air campaign evolved. Gone were the days of large alpha strike packages with wave after wave of attack aircraft rolling onto a target. The advent of precision-guide munitions and improved bombing efficiency meant fewer strike aircraft, but the higher threat environment required an ever-growing cast of supporting aircraft. Thus, it was all about protecting the strike force and it was not uncommon for a typical Air Force strike package to consist of a strike flight of some two dozen F-4s equipped with precision munitions and conventional bombs to be supported by upward of 65 aircraft to jam radars and confuse ground controllers, counter SAM threats, suppress anti-aircraft fire, and protect against marauding MiGs.[22] In addition, each mission would be assigned a complete complement of

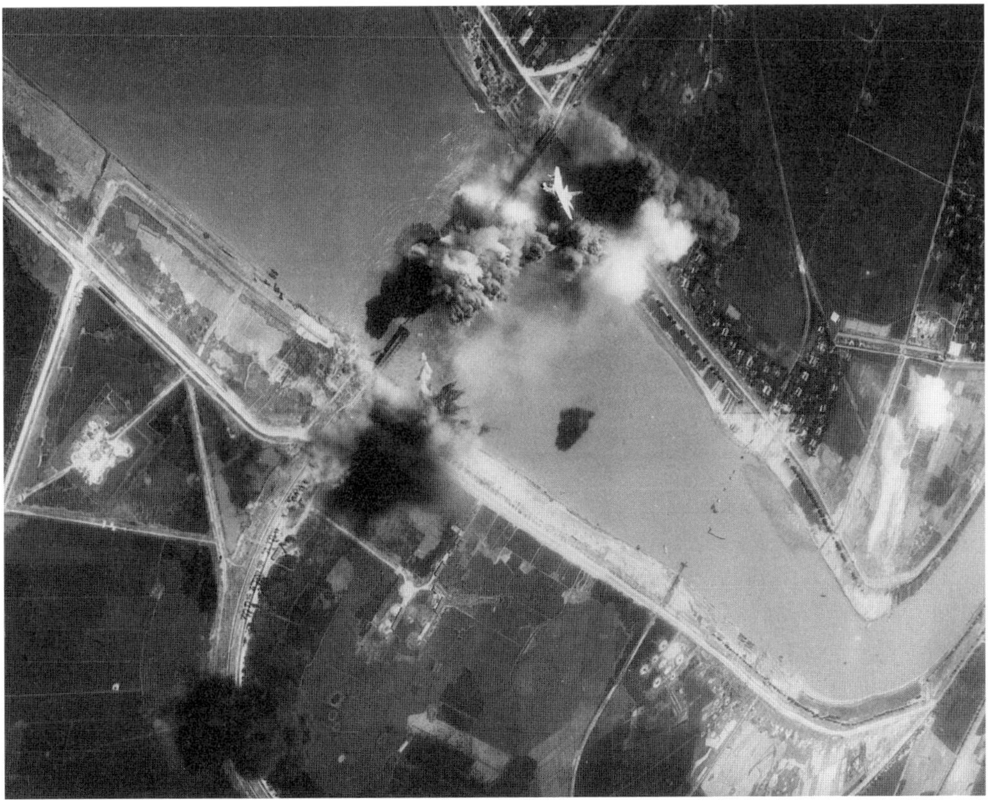

An A-7E from VA-195 striking the Hai Duong bridge chokepoint linking Hanoi and Haiphong, May 1972. (Photo U.S. Navy)

aircraft providing search and rescue capability, aerial tanker support, and airborne surveillance and communication capability. Not surprisingly, this high level of effort would severely tax both men and machines throughout the course of the campaign.

Operation Pocket Money

A key to stopping Hanoi's offensive in the South lay in the ability of the United States to significantly slow the flow of men, equipment, and supplies to the battlefield, but past American air interdiction campaigns had been only marginally successful and the ongoing Freedom Train operations alone were unlikely to produce the desired outcome unless something dramatically different was done.

American military planners had long recognized the limitations of strategic interdiction as long as the North Vietnamese had an open-ended and uninterrupted source of supply from outside the country. In particular, Hanoi's war machine was heavily dependent on resupply by sea and nearly 85 percent of the North's imports—including practically all its oil shipments—came by sea, mainly from the Soviet Union and Eastern Europe. Moreover, virtually all of Hanoi's sophisticated military equipment from surface-to-air missiles, fighter aircraft, and air defense equipment to tanks and heavy artillery flowed through the Haiphong docks, making the port a critical chokepoint. Accordingly, a blockade of Haiphong and of other smaller North Vietnamese ports through the sowing of minefields would likely have a profound impact on the North's ability to prosecute the war. Thus, Operation Pocket Money was born.

An A-7E from VA-22 is loaded with Mk 52 sea mines on the eve of the mining of Haiphong harbor in May 1972 as part of Operation Pocket Money. (Photo U.S. Navy)

While militarily sound, a mining blockade of North Vietnamese ports was a risky political proposition. It put "neutral" communist-flagged ships in danger and, moreover, it could draw the Soviet Union directly into the conflict at a time when Washington was seeking to improve relations and get the Kremlin's help in advancing the Paris peace talks. It might also backfire and spur greater Chinese military aid to Hanoi to counter the American blockade. Nonetheless, Nixon bit the bullet and authorized the mining of North Vietnamese ports on May 5.

On the morning of May 8, six Navy A-7s and three Marine A-6s launched from the deck of the USS *Coral Sea* carrying at total of 36 Mk 52 1,000-pound electromagnetic mines to sow the first minefield in the main shipping channel into Haiphong. The mission plan called for a quick run in with all nine aircraft dropping their mines in a single pass to avoid the anticipated heavy anti-aircraft fire from shore batteries. To maintain the element of surprise other Navy planes would launch diversionary strikes away from Haiphong, while ECM jammers and fighter escorts screened the attack force. Two guided-missile cruisers, the USS *Chicago* and USS *Long Beach*, were also moved into position off the coast to provide radar warning coverage and defensive missile fire should North Vietnamese fighters react. Despite all these preparations, it would be a tricky mission that would test the skill and nerve of the pilots, who were all dropping aerial mines in combat for the first time.

Skimming just 50 feet above the water to avoid radar detection and negate the SAM threat, the heavily laden jets made a beeline for the harbor channel shortly before 0900. Suddenly the *Chicago*'s radar picked up four enemy fighters heading southeast from Hanoi toward the strike force. The cruiser quickly fired a salvo of Talos surface-to-air missiles at the enemy formation, downing one MiG and forcing the others to scatter. Meanwhile, the strike force pressed on against light and not very accurate anti-aircraft fire and within the space of a few minutes all 36 mines were in the water without the loss of any aircraft. The mines would self-activate within 72 hours and nine ships took advantage of the departure warning but 27 others found themselves trapped in the harbor.

Even before the pilots touched down on the deck of the *Coral Sea*, President Nixon was informing the American public of the mining of Haiphong harbor in a televised address and of his decision to begin a new, intense strategic bombing campaign against North Vietnam. Nixon noted that he'd reluctantly taken these actions in response to Hanoi's continuing offensive in South Vietnam and its refusal to negotiate an acceptable settlement to the war. The time for talking was over and during the course of the next several weeks Navy aircraft closed off the rest of North Vietnam's sea routes, dropping nearly 11,000 500-pound Mk 36 Destructor mines into the smaller ports of Cam Pha and Hoi Gai north of Haiphong, as well as in the river estuaries at Thanh Hoa, Vinh, Quang Khe, and Dong Hoi. The war in the North had certainly reached a new phase.

Adapted from S. Emerson, *Vietnam's Final Air Campaign*, pp. 44-47, 58.

Tightening the Screws

The frenetic pace of Linebacker continued unabated into the summer as more men and planes were thrown into America's ever-expanding air campaign that not only targeted critical elements of the North Vietnamese transportation and logistics network, but also sought to permanently degrade the North's war-making and defensive capabilities through the wholesale destruction of its military-industrial infrastructure and thus, force Hanoi to return to the negotiating table.

With the early May closure of the North Vietnamese ports, the country was now entirely dependent on overland routes from China to meet its nearly 150,000 tons per month of imports. The two rail lines and eight major roads out of China, which had previously carried only 15 percent of supply requirements,[23] were now forced to carry the entire burden. It was up to the 8th TFW to close down these routes or at least make resupply as difficult and time-consuming as possible by repeatedly bombing key chokepoints that included bridges and major road segments. Thanks to the use of precision-guided munitions, General Vogt would be able to claim that "we had 15 bridges out on each railroad at any given time—as fast as they would build them, we would knock them

Classic star-shaped, surface-to-air missile site: SA-2 missile launchers positioned around the perimeter and communications and command vans in the center; Fan Song guidance radar located in upper left. (Photo National Museum of the U.S. Air Force)

out again."[24] Not only was the bombing effective, but it had become much more efficient: five bridges were destroyed in one day using 24 laser-guided bombs, a feat that likely would likely have required more than 2,000 unguided bombs during Rolling Thunder.[25]

The assault on the transportation and logistics network extended well beyond the Chinese rail and road corridors. South and east of the capital and along the rail and road corridor from Thanh Hoa all the way down to Dong Hoi, Navy aircraft kept the pressure on. Typical of this effort was the 33-plane alpha strike launched by the USS *Saratoga* against the rail and highway bridge over the Song Day River at Phu Ly, about 40 miles south of Hanoi. In the face of heavy anti-aircraft fire, A-7s and A-6s were able to heavily damage both bridges with Walleye electro-optically guided bombs, as well as destroy an estimated 75 percent of the nearby military storage area with conventional bombs.[26] Continuous strikes by naval aircraft against the Thanh Hoa, Vinh, and the Dong Hoi logistics hubs throughout June and July were also effective in disrupting the movement of men and matériel southward and hampering repair efforts.

By the end of June the Air Force alone claimed to have destroyed more than 100 bridges and intelligence analysts estimated that there was no uncut stretch of the North Vietnamese rail system longer than 50 miles.[27] Thus, trucks now began to assume a major role in the North's transportation calculus with U.S. intelligence estimating that the North Vietnamese had more than 20,000 trucks in its inventory in 1972.[28] Not surprisingly, as the successful bridge-busting effort continued there was a significant surge in trucks carrying supplies as rail lines and rail bridges were rendered inoperable. At one point aerial reconnaissance identified up to 40 trucks per mile along the highway paralleling the northeast rail line from China to Hanoi.[29] While some effort was made to

Bristling with anti-aircraft guns, surface-to-air missiles, and MiG fighter aircraft, the North Vietnamese capital had become one of the best-defended cities in the world by 1972. (Photo National Museum of the U.S. Air Force)

attack these truck convoys, the old method of flying armed reconnaissance missions in the operational areas encompassing Hanoi and Haiphong was deemed too high risk with marginal reward. Instead General Vogt opted to disrupt the truck traffic by destroying highway bridges and attacking vehicle storage areas, truck repair facilities, and supply staging areas.

The North's southern panhandle also saw a marked uptick in bombing activity during the summer as well. With the U.S. B-52 inventory in Southeast Asia rising to 206 by the end of June, more of the big bombers could now be diverted away from the battlefields in South Vietnam. On June 8, B-52s carried out their first Linebacker missions striking troop concentrations and supply depots in the Dong Hoi area and would go on to log 260 sorties that month and then average 30 sorties per day over the panhandle through the remainder of the air campaign.[30] The Navy, now with up to six carriers on station in the Gulf of Tonkin, likewise upped the tempo by hammering away at bridges, coastal barges, truck convoys, and supply depots from Haiphong to the DMZ.

In conjunction with the strategic interdiction campaign, strikes were also launched against important industrial facilities, POL storage sites, and key military installations and airfields across the North in an effort to degrade Hanoi's war-making and

The North's transportation network supplying its forces in the South was a central focus of American aerial interdiction efforts. (Photo National Museum of the U.S. Air Force)

defensive capabilities. High-profile targets included Hanoi's main electric transformer station, the Thai Nguyen industrial complex, the Bac Giang thermal power plant, and Haiphong's POL storage facilities, as well as Hanoi's Bac Mai air defense and command center and the MiG airfields at Kep, Phuc Yen, and Yen Bai. Yet none was more telling than the June 10 destruction of the North's newest and largest hydroelectric facility at Lang Chi, about 65 miles northwest of Hanoi along the Red River. On that day, 12 Air Force F-4s out of Ubon launched a highly choreographed strike on the facility by first blasting an opening through the plant's concrete roof and then dropping time-delayed laser-guided munitions through the hole to destroy the plant's four turbine generators.[31] All this was accomplished without inflicting any collateral damage to the off-limits dam upon which the power plant rested.

American pilots were now flying up to 300 Linebacker sorties per day with great impact. North Vietnamese imports for June were reduced from 160,000 tons to a mere 30,000 tons and the port blockade and destruction of the oil pipeline from China had effectively cut off all new oil imports.[32] Moreover, American bombing had destroyed some 25 percent of country's main POL reserves, creating a growing countrywide fuel shortage. The impact on the southern battlefield was also telling with General Vogt estimating that the flow of supplies southward by July was cut by at least 20 percent and the enemy in South Vietnam was experiencing rising shortages of fuel, food, and ammunition.[33] Admiral McCain as Commander-in-Chief Pacific forces further underscored that the full impact of the bombing would become even more apparent as North Vietnamese stockpiles and supply caches in the South were depleted.[34]

Toward a Turning Point

None of these successes could have been accomplished without a determined American effort to target, degrade, and defeat the North's air defenses from the onset of the campaign. While advancements in technology, aircraft and avionics, unit specialization, and a maturation of operational tactics gave U.S. forces a distinct advantage, the North Vietnamese sought to negate many of these advantages as best they could to weather the storm and ultimately outlast the Americans—just as they had done in the past. It would be just as much a psychological and political battle, as it was a military one.

Despite suffering heavy fighter losses on the opening day of Linebacker, the North Vietnamese strategy appeared to be effective at inflicting casualties and keeping the Americans off balance into the summer. A highly effective early warning radar network and aggressive MiG-21 pilots using coordinated hit-and-run tactics claimed another 13 Air Force F-4s in June and July in the skies over Hanoi, while losing only seven of their own planes.[35] The highly maneuverable MiGs, equipped with 23-mm and 30-mm cannons, gave them an edge in close-in dogfighting, especially against Air Force F-4s armed only with air-to-air missiles.

It was a situation that the top Air Force leadership moved quickly to address. A vastly improved MiG warning system (call sign "Teaball") was established utilizing an orbiting EC-121 and changes were made to improve intelligence collection and communications. Most significantly, the Seventh Air Force in Thailand instituted operational changes,

U.S. Air Force F-111s on the taxiway at Takhil air base in Thailand. (Photo National Museum of the U.S. Air Force)

whereby entire wings would specialize in a single mission component—bombing (8th TFW), combat air patrol (432nd TRW), or escort duties (388th TFW)—that allowed pilots and air crews to gain expertise and experience more quickly. Other changes included the establishment of the Red Flag combat exercise program at Nellis Air Force Base to closely mimic the Navy's highly successful Top Gun dogfighting school, the development of the AIM-7 "dogfight Sparrow" with a more effective minimum range, and increased inventories of F-4Es with a built-in 20-mm nose cannon that gave Air Force pilots another close-in dogfighting weapon.

These changes, as well as the VPAF's continuing loss of experienced pilots and planes, would steadily diminish the MiG threat by August. In the final three months of the campaign only five Air Force aircraft would be lost to MiGs, while the kill-to-loss ratio would steadily rise to 4:1 in the Air Force's favor, matching Rolling Thunder's peak performance.[36] This period would also see the first Air Force ace on August 28 when Captain Richard "Steve" Ritchie scored his fifth MiG kill. He would later be joined by two others, captains Charles DeBellevue and Jeffery Feinstein in September and October.

As the air-to-air threat decreased, the Air Force and Navy moved increasingly to neutralize the threat from the ground. The advent of precision-guided munitions and

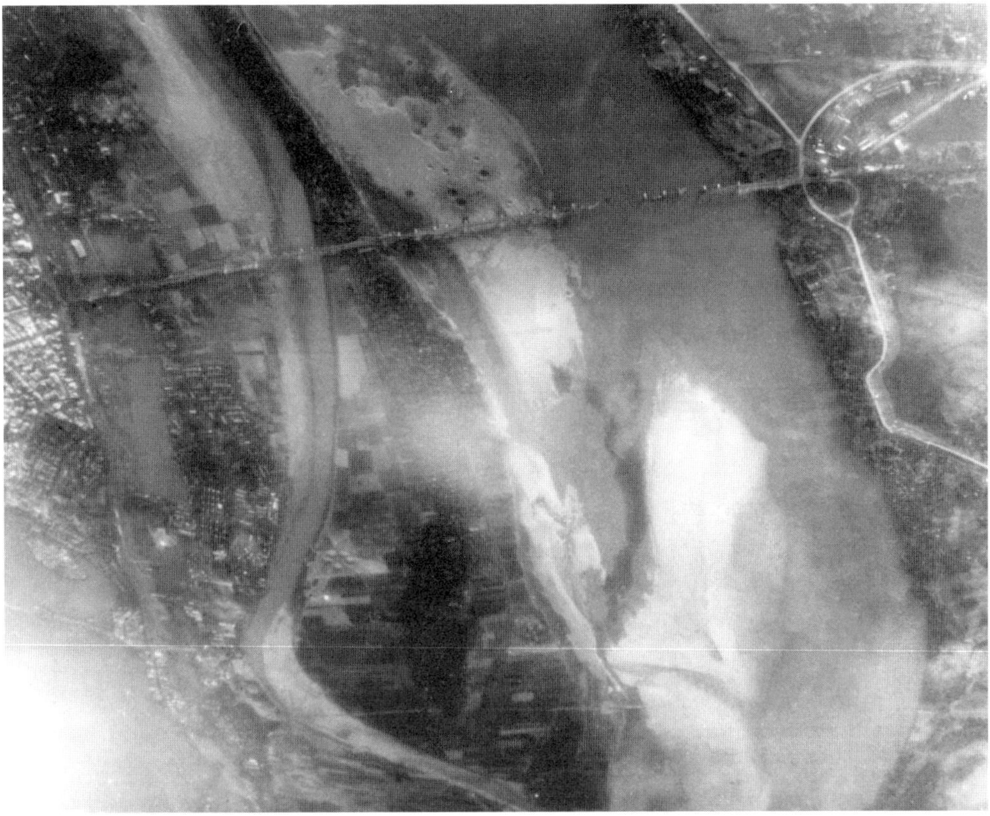

Hanoi's important Paul Doumer Bridge over the Red River would fall victim to U.S. Air Force laser-guided bombs in the opening days of the air campaign.

advanced computer bombing and navigation systems in Navy aircraft, like the A-6 and the A-7E, not only increased the accuracy of U.S. bombing, but put fewer strike aircraft at risk over the target. Moreover, the ability to release payloads at greater altitude and distance from the target enabled American pilots to avoid the curtain of protective anti-aircraft fire that had claimed so many aircraft during Rolling Thunder. The North's more modern, radar-guided 85-mm and 100-mm guns could still shoot down even the highest attacking aircraft, but the introduction of more capable electronic counter-measures went a long way in mitigating this threat.

It was the surface-to-air threat posed by the North's SA-2 missile batteries that quickly emerged as the biggest ground-fire threat to American planes during Linebacker—accounting for the loss of 24 aircraft[37]—and it was the struggle to defeat this leg of Hanoi's air defense triad that soon became the centerpiece of U.S. striking planning efforts.

All Air Force and Navy strike packages relied on an assortment of aircraft electronic countermeasures to jam or confuse enemy tracking radars and the SA-2 guidance radars. These included airborne platforms, like the Air Force's old standby EB-66 or the Navy's new EA-6 Prowler, to newer jamming pods carried by individual planes. Sometimes, however, the simplest countermeasures were the best; the Air Force made extensive and highly effective use of chaff corridors to mask their strike aircraft when approaching targets. Every U.S. countermeasure, however, would elicit an enemy response, such as shifting radar frequencies or wavelengths, which then needed to be countered as each side sought to negate the other's technology.

In addition, Navy A-6 and A-7 Iron Hands and Air Force F-105G Wild Weasels were an essential component of strike packages in 1972 and the most effective tool for suppressing SAM sites. Although the Iron Hand concept of using radar homing missiles to destroy the site's guidance radar had been around since 1965, it had seen considerable evolution both in terms of improved missiles with greater range and larger warheads, as well as updated tactics by the time of the Linebacker raids. The latter included the Air Force's creation of "hunter-killer" teams. This involved two F-105G Wild Weasels working in tandem with two F-4Es to not only destroy the radar with a missile hit, but also to completely pulverize the entire site with Mk 20 cluster bombs dropped by the Phantoms. By the end of August, the hunter-killer teams had proven highly valuable in forcing the North Vietnamese to modify their tactics, move their launchers more frequently, and pay more attention to camouflaging their sites. As a result of these combined passive and active countermeasures, the effectiveness of the North's surface-to-air missile threat was vastly reduced—averaging only one kill per 150 missiles fired—by the end of the campaign.[38]

Not only was the military situation beginning to turn in Washington's favor by mid-summer, but the political failure of Hanoi's allies—Moscow and Beijing—to stridently denounce the bombing campaign and come to the aid of North Vietnam forced Le Duan's hand. Even as the American bombing continued, Kissinger and Tho returned to the negotiating table to try and hammer out a peace settlement. While steady progress was made, numerous sticking points, such the presence of North Vietnamese troops in the South after an American withdrawal, the future of U.S. military assistance to Saigon, and demands for the removal of President Thieu from power, were proving difficult to resolve.[39] Moreover, the talks did not spell an end to Linebacker, as Nixon did not want to repeat the mistakes of 1968 by easing off the military pressure during negotiations until a firm settlement was in hand. While the air campaign was accomplishing both its military and political goals, it did come at a cost for the Americans, with 73 aircraft shot down by the end of August.

North Vietnamese MiG-21 pilots proved to be more than a match for American fighter pilots in the opening months of the air campaign. (Photo National Museum of the U.S. Air Force)

5. SAIGON COUNTERATTACKS

As the air began to clear over the battlefields around Hue, An Loc, and Kontum by mid-June, Saigon and Washington could breathe a sigh of relief. They had survived. Disaster had been averted. But still there was much to do to tip the military balance back in the South Vietnamese favor and it would be a long and arduous task to retake the territory lost to the enemy. Nonetheless, there was a growing sense of optimism and confidence among the Saigon's new fighting generals that they and their men were up to the challenge.

Progress, however, would be much slower than expected over the next three months and the results much more muted than anticipated. Having troops stand tall in defense was one thing, pushing forward in the teeth of fierce enemy resistance was entirely another matter. There was little choice. President Thieu's political needs outweighed any military rational: it was completely unacceptable for his government to allow the North Vietnamese territorial gains to stand. Moreover, failure to take the fight to the enemy would likely further undermine faith in Vietnamization and serve to erode Saigon's negotiating position in the peace talks. The die was cast: Saigon's forces were going over to the attack.

The trek back north to Quang Tri city would prove to be a tough slog for General Truong's troops in the face of determined communist resistance.

Breaking Out from the Hue Pocket

From a symbolic and military perspective, the recapture of Quang Tri Province and its provincial capital was the top priority of the government's upcoming counteroffensive and General Truong, as the new I Corps commander, was just the right man for the job. Since mid-May, I Corps troops had been conducting aggressive spoiling attacks against the North Vietnamese forces encircling Hue. These operations were not only successful in disrupting enemy offensive preparations and keeping him off balance, but they instilled a renewed sense of confidence in Truong's men and paved the way for a general offensive in late June.

The offensive—codenamed Lam Son 72—got underway on June 28 with a two-pronged assault northward across the My Chanh River by Airborne and the Marine troops that was preceded by intense air, artillery, and naval bombardment. The Airborne Division's three brigades were tasked with sweeping up the west side of Highway 1 and skirting the old fire support base Nancy toward the Thanh Han River to arrive at a position just south of Quang Tri city. Simultaneously, the Marine Division supported by the 1st Ranger Group and the 7th Armored Cavalry would push up coastal Route 555 (the infamous "Street without Joy" from the First Indochina War) and approach Quang Tri city from the southeast. While retaking the provincial capital was politically imperative for President Thieu, General Truong saw his primary objective as "first to destroy enemy forces ... bypass[ing] political objectives ... unless it became necessary to destroy the enemy."[1]

An ARVN M48 tank advancing under the cover of a U.S. F-4 air strike.

To secure Hue and his rear area, the 1st ARVN Division would assault southwest of the Hue pocket to disrupt NVA forces and drive them further back from the city, while the 2d ARVN Division would conduct search-and-destroy operations in Quang Tin and Quang Ngai provinces farther to the south. The now-reconstituted 3d Division would provide protection for the logistics base and airfield at Da Nang. Thus, with Hue and his lines of communication secure, Truong could focus completely on rooting out and eliminating North Vietnamese forces in Quang Tri Province. If successful, the offensive would completely overturn the communist gains of April and May and inflict a devastating blow on Hanoi's already weakened troops in MR 1.

Progress was initially good after breaching the North Vietnamese defenses north of the My Chanh River for the Airborne Division's thrust north before it ran into more determined resistance as the North Vietnamese to fell back toward Quang Tri city and the Thach Han River. The three Marines brigades to the east of Highway 1, however, encountered tough going from the start as they tried to dislodge dug-in elements of the 304th NVA Division along the coast. An amphibious landing by two Marine battalions at Wunder Beach behind the enemy defenses on June 29 outflanked the defenders, forcing them to fall back northward. By the end of June, it was estimated that offensive operations had killed more than 1,500 North Vietnamese and destroyed nearly two dozen armored vehicles.[2]

Thanks to heavy tactical air support, Truong's western thrust made slow, but steady progress and on July 7 elements of the 2d Airborne Brigade reached the outskirts of Quang Tri after more than a week of hard fighting. Here the paratroopers encountered a well-entrenched enemy supported by artillery and mortars. After two weeks of tough fighting the paratroopers were rebuffed in their repeated attempts to capture the city's citadel, although they came within several hundred yards of capturing their objective. This setback was made even worse because this followed President Thieu's premature claim that the city been retaken. Hanoi, for its part, seized the opportunity to pour reinforcements from the 325C NVA and 312th NVA divisions into the defense of the city and even launch some limited counterattacks against the Airborne Division. It was increasingly apparent to all that the North Vietnamese were determined to make a stand at Quang Tri and force the South Vietnamese into grueling urban warfare.

In the meantime, the Marines were making a concerted effort to cut the enemy's supply lines to the northeast of the city along Route 560 and push the enemy back toward the Cua Viet River. An initial helicopter assault on July 11 proved successful, yet costly when one of the U.S. Marine CH-53 helicopters transporting part of a battalion of South Vietnamese Marines was downed by a shoulder-fired surface-to-air missile. Forty-two Marines died in the crash, two of them Americans, in the first U.S. Marine aircraft lost to an SA-7.[3] Two additional helicopters were lost to ground fire and another 28 sustained damage, but the Marines prevailed in the firefight, capturing the position and killing 126 of the enemy. The Marines suffered over 150 casualties, but were able to sever the road by mid-July.[4] A follow-on assault on July 22 by the 147th Marine Brigade supported by tanks was also successful in pushing the enemy back toward the Cua Viet River and further isolating Quang Tri.

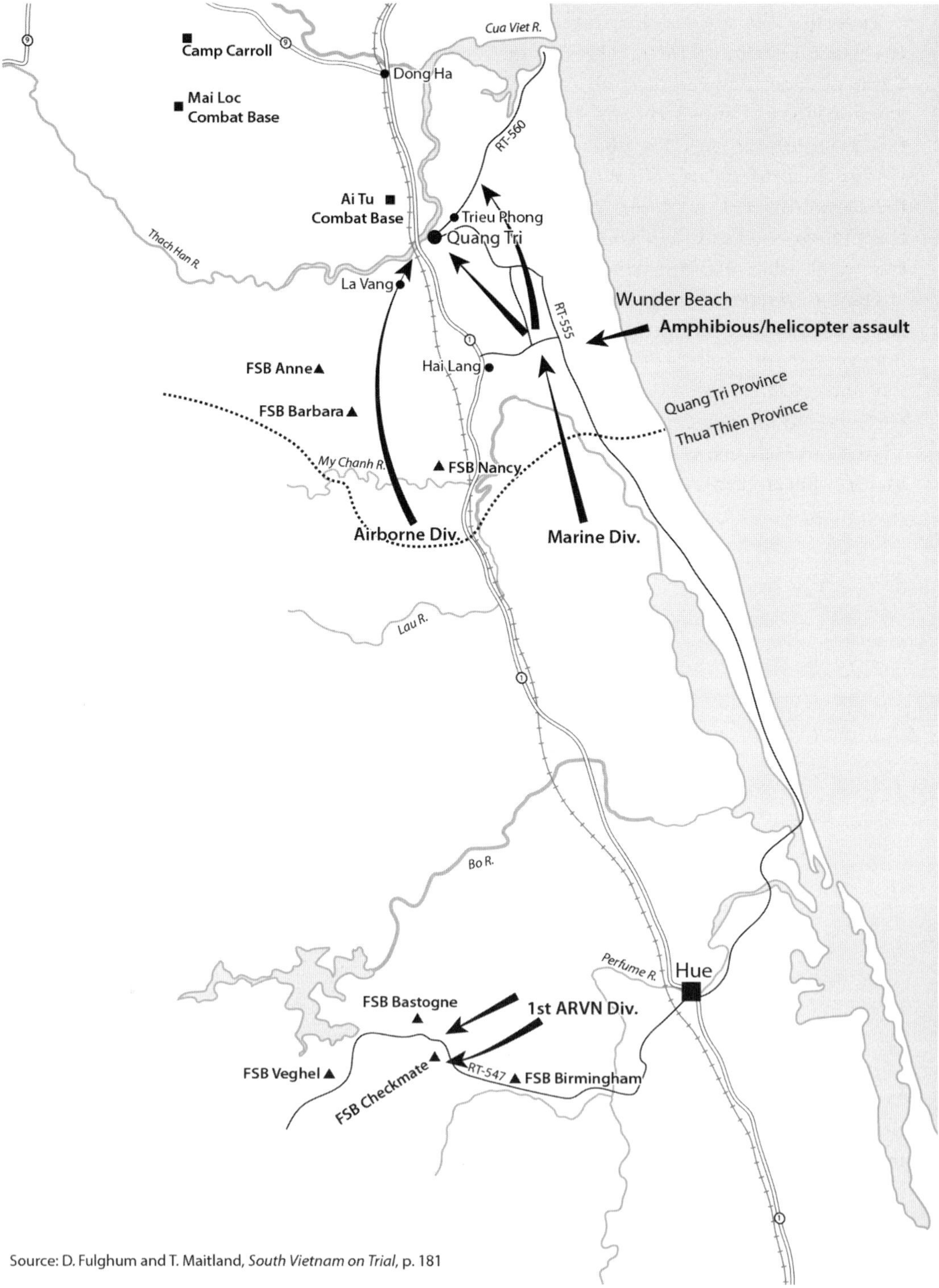

Source: D. Fulghum and T. Maitland, *South Vietnam on Trial*, p. 181

Map 8: Recapturing Quang Tri.

Then the offensive stalled. The Airborne troops were spent and their ranks thinned from near-constant fighting since April after being rushed from one crisis to the next. General Truong found himself at a crossroads with not only Saigon, but the world, watching his next move. He modified his original plans by replacing the battered Airborne troops on July 27 with Brigadier General Bui Thi Lan's Marines, whose new assignment was to recapture Quang Tri city. The Rangers would take over the coastal flank, while the newly relieved paratroopers would cover the Marines' western flank and safeguard the Highway 1 supply line to Hue. And although Truong was keen to avoid the bloody specter of urban warfare, the North Vietnamese decision to make their defensive stand at Quang Tri gave him "the opportunity to accomplish my mission [by] employing the superior firepower of our American ally."[5] Soon wave after wave of tactical aircraft and B-52s began unleashing their payloads on and around the city, pounding the defenders day and night. In July alone, U.S. aircraft would fly nearly 7,500 tactical and Arc Light sorties[6]—the largest single-month total of the Easter Offensive—in MR 1 with the North Vietnamese suffering almost 2,000 dead.[7] But still Hanoi's men continued to hold out under the ever-growing pile of rumble that was once a city.

Aerial photo showing the devastation to the center of An Loc with damaged and destroyed vehicles and tanks highlighted, June 1972. (Photo National Museum of the U.S. Air Force)

While the fight around Quang Tri raged, the 1st ARVN Division southwest of Hue was encountering its own set of problems as it attempted to clear the area of the threat posed by the 324B NVA Division in Thua Thien Province. Enemy activity along Route 547 had increased substantially and by July fire base Checkmate had changed hands several times and Bastogne was once again overrun as the 1st Division neared exhaustion after five months of hard fighting. With the addition of a regiment from the 3d ARVN Division and increased tactical and Arc Light strikes, both firebases were recaptured by August and offensive probes continued to drive the battered remnants of the 324B Division westward.

Likewise, enemy activity in the three southernmost provinces of MR 1 also increased as the North Vietnamese sought to divert Saigon's forces away from Quang Tri city by threatening anew I Corps' lines of communication south of Da Nang in Quang Nam Province. Several heavy attacks were launched in late June and July against elements of the 2d ARVN Division in Que Son Valley and along the Song Ly Ly River. The river valley was only about 30 miles southwest of Da Nang and the vital Highway 1 supply line and was the scene of several bloody clashes between U.S Marines and communist forces back in 1967/68. The vital air base at Da Nang was also repeatedly rocketed in August with the attack on the night of August 17/18 destroying an O-2A FAC aircraft and an HH-53 helicopter and damaging another ten aircraft.[8] Meanwhile, a growing threat by the 2d NVA Division in the far south of MR 1 forced the 2d ARVN Division commander to shift his attention to Quang Ngai Province. This required the 3d ARVN Division to counter the enemy buildup in the Que Son Valley and parts of Quang Tin Province and in its first combat operations since its reconstitution, the 3d Division performed well in retaking the district capital of Tien Phuoc. As the summer wore on, the 2d and 3d divisions were able to gain the upper hand in the three southern provinces of MR 1 with the North Vietnamese steadily withdrawing westward to regroup and refit.

Forward Air Controllers: Low, Slow and in Harm's Way

The massive and extensive use of air power in helping stem the tide of the North Vietnam's Easter Offensive would come to be a defining theme of the campaign, but one that often overlooked the vital role played by forward air controllers or FACs in helping to secure battlefield victory in the face of looming disaster.

Flying at low levels at slow speed, light aircraft like the O-1 Bird Dog, O-2A Skymaster or the OV-10 Bronco, American and South Vietnamese FACs had become by 1972 highly adept at locating and marking enemy targets with smoke or white phosphorus rockets and then directing and coordinating air strikes. From attack helicopters and fixed-wing gunships to prop-driven A-1 Skyraiders and fast attack jets, the orbiting FACs were the essential mechanism for delivering aerial firepower in the most timely and accurate manner possible. It was, however, their determination and bravery during the most intense battles of the Easter Offensive, including the defense of Hue, Kontum, and An Loc, that brought them into their own and helped guarantee their legacy. It would come at the cost of 16 aircraft and the lives of eight pilots and crew with Air Force Captain Steven Bennett being posthumously awarded the Congressional Medal of Honor for his actions on June 29, 1972.

Flying the OV-10 Bronco and other small aircraft, forward air controllers (FACs) braved intense enemy fire to coordinate and directed American and South Vietnamese air strikes. (Photo National Museum of the U.S. Air Force)

At the outbreak of fighting in the spring, the men and aircraft of the U.S. Air Force's 20th Tactical Air Support Squadron (TASS) at Da Nang and the 21st TASS at Tan Son Nhut outside Saigon were called upon to render desperately needed close air support to the embattled South Vietnamese troops in Quang Tri and Binh Long provinces under the most difficult conditions. In addition to coordinating air strikes, FACs also helped direct naval gunfire support in defense of government positions along the northern coast. Low cloud ceilings and generally poor visibility often complicated their missions, which were made increasingly dangerous by the large numbers of North Vietnamese anti-aircraft weapons and surface-to-air missiles brought onto the battlefield. Two OV-10s and an O-2A would be lost to enemy ground fire and missiles over Quang Tri Province in the opening week of the campaign and another three aircraft were shot down near An Loc in May.

The Air Force FACs really earned their stripes and the respect of ground troops over May and June during the defense of the Hue pocket, An Loc, and Kontum. Braving heavy ground fire and SA-7 missiles, they often maintained a near round-the-clock presence at a mere 5,000 to 7,000 feet over the battlefield to help shatter mass infantry assaults and advancing tanks with wave after wave of aircraft. In dire situations where no immediate air support was available, FAC pilots would frequently roll in and rake enemy troops with machine-gun and rocket fire and even make fake strafing runs when all their ammunition had exhausted to disrupt attacks.

Often unheralded and overlooked in the history books, the forward air controller component of American and South Vietnamese air power contributed enormously to the air attack's effectiveness: at least half the enemy killed and some 450 tanks destroyed were believed to be the result of air strikes.

Stabilizing the South

With the lifting of the siege of An Loc in mid-June, the weary defenders began the arduous task of mopping up the last remaining pockets of resistance surrounding the city, while other units sought to secure the city's supply lines to the south. There was also, however, time to celebrate their victory. On July 7, President Thieu and General Minh flew unannounced into the city to survey the battlefield and praise General Hung and his men for their valiant defense by saying, it was not just the symbol of their victory over the North Vietnamese, but rather it was a larger "victory of the Free World over the theory of people's war [and the] revolutionary war of world communism."[9] Fresh troops were also brought in in mid-July. The 18th ARVN Division relieved the depleted and ravaged 5th Division at An Loc, while the 25th ARVN Division took over from the 21st Division and assumed the former's mission of reopening Route 13 by clearing the enemy blocking position at Tau O. The 25th Division troops were able to root out the defenders and by July 20 the road from Lai Khe to An Loc was completely open, but travel remained somewhat risky as the road was still subject to shelling by North Vietnamese artillery and some portions still needed to be demined. The 18th Division, however, made less progress in its efforts to recapture the Quan Loi airfield east of An Loc. Despite government gains throughout August, North Vietnamese troops still clung to the high ground north of the airstrip well into September.

As the fighting in MR 3 began to wane in mid-summer, Saigon turned its attention toward the Mekong Delta region, where enemy activity had been on the increase.

South Vietnamese Marines would bear the brunt of the effort to recapture Quang Tri city from July to September 1972.

While much of the fighting in the early months of the Easter Offensive in this region centered on the western provinces and across the northern border into Cambodia, by early June elements of the 5th NVA Division began to redeploy from the An Loc area to the Parrot's Beak salient separating MR 3 and the Delta's MR 4. These forces were apparently moving to support the 1st NVA Division in Cambodia, as well as several Viet Cong regiments newly active in the eastern portions of MR 4. Responding aggressively, IV Corps commander Major General Nguyen Vinh Nghi launched a series of strikes into the Parrot's Beak salient. Catching the communist forces off guard as they prepared to infiltrate into MR 4, the 7th ARVN Division along with tactical air support and B-52 strikes inflicted heavy losses on the enemy.[10] After nearly three weeks of fighting, Saigon's forces were in complete control of the area.

While the 7th Division was engaged across the border in Cambodia, Viet Cong regiments in early July escalated their attacks in Dinh Tuong Province and were joined by two regiments of the 5th VC Division, increasing pressure on the vital Route 4 that linked the Delta's main rice-producing area to Saigon. Fortunately, the release of the 15th ARVN Regiment of the 9th Division from duty at An Loc and the redeployment of two Ranger groups stymied the enemy's efforts. Once again B-52 Arc Light strikes were used to pummel suspected enemy base areas in the Plain of Reeds near the Cao Lanh area of Kien Phong Province. Nonetheless, the North Vietnamese continued to push additional

Desperate civilians scamper to board a South Vietnamese helicopter during a lull in the fighting at An Loc, June 1972.

men into the area east of the Mekong River, but the return of the 21st ARVN Division and additional Ranger battalion reinforcements enabled General Nghi to check the enemy infiltration. And in early August Ranger forces were able to inflict a stinging defeat on the enemy just north of My Tho in eastern Dinh Tuong Province that not only effectively ended the threat to MR 4, but allowed government forces by September to reestablish control over formerly communist-occupied areas of the Delta.

Securing the Central Highlands

As the last of the enemy soldiers were cleared from Kontum and the city's immediate surroundings on June 10, an eerie calm fell over the Central Highlands as both sides caught their breathe and took stock of their situation after months of hard and bloody fighting. A few days earlier, the North Vietnamese Central Highlands command concluded that "the conditions for completely annihilating the enemy no longer existed [and] decided to order a pullback."[11] Surviving elements of the 320th NVA Division pulled back to the Tan Canh–Dak To II area along Route 512 to regroup and refit, while the 2nd NVA Division withdrew northward back to its jungle stronghold in neighboring Quang Ngai Province to lick its wounds. Apart from some minor patrolling activity, Brigadier General Ba was content to give his men a well-deserved rest too.

The 23d ARVN Division's rest was short-lived, however, as General Toan pushed Ba to launch clearing operations north and northwest of Kontum in the second half of June to recover lost territory and pursue retreating enemy forces. These had some localized success, but the weakened state of the division and the lack of reinforcements prevented any significant advance up Route 14 toward Vo Dinh. Several airmobile raids into the Tan Canh sector over the summer kept the enemy off balance and in a defensive posture, but the raids were unable to produce any lasting benefits given the inability of government forces to follow up with sustained offensive operations. Thus, the battle lines stabilized with the northern two-thirds of Kontum Province in communist hands, while Saigon's forces remained in firm control of Kontum city and the bulk of the province's population.

More significant fighting took place to the south of Kontum along Route 14 in the second half of June as ARVN forces sought to clear the North Vietnamese blocking force at Chu Pao Pass. Over the course of the next several weeks battalion after battalion was thrown against the well-entrenched enemy, who put up a stout resistance despite heavy casualties and dwindling supplies. On June 26, South Vietnamese troops finally took the high ground on both sides of the pass and forced the surviving North Vietnamese to retreat. The Pleiku–Kontom road was declared open to military convoys on June 30 and a week later civilian traffic began to flow, although vehicles were subject to periodic harassing attacks throughout the remainder of the summer.

Over on the coast in Binh Dinh Province, the 41st Regiment of the 22d ARVN Division had been weathering a last-ditch North Vietnamese effort in early June to seize control of the critical province. Sitting astride Highway 1 and just 30 miles north of the provincial capital of Qui Nhon, the regiment's defensive position at Landing Zone Crystal was all that stood between the communist forces severing central Vietnam in two. For five days the North Vietnamese troops rained down artillery and mortar fire on the defenders and

U.S. Marine CH-34 helicopters from the USS *Okinawa* and other amphibious ships were used extensively by South Vietnamese Marines to air-assault behind enemy lines in Quang Tri Province.

an all-out infantry assault by 3d NVA Division troops on June 4/5 nearly succeeded in overrunning the position. The timely arrival of AC-130 gunships, tactical air strikes, and well-directed naval gunfire finally quashed the attack. Following their defeat and heavy losses, the enemy withdrew.

Despite President Thieu's demand for quick action in retaking the previously lost districts and major towns in the north of Binh Dinh Province, it would be mid-July before the offensive got off the ground. Colonel Phan Dinh Niem, the 22d Division commander, first had to relocate his headquarters back to Qui Nhon from Pleiku and then organize the redeployment of his two regiments at Pleiku to join the 41st Regiment on the coast. The counteroffensive finally got underway on July 19 with the 22d Division driving up the coast, while the 6th Ranger Group advanced northeast from Kontum. Rather than face this formidable force and accompanying air power, the 3d NVA Division wisely retreated northward, leaving behind a modest rearguard of Viet Cong troops to slow the advance. Against this feeble resistance the district capital of Hoai Nhon was retaken on July 21, Tam Quan on July 23, and Hoai An three days later. By August the situation in Binh Dinh had largely returned to its pre-Easter Offensive status: communist forces firmly ensconced in the rugged An Lao Valley away from the coast, but still posing a threat, while Saigon's forces maintained control over the major towns along the coastal plain, as well as over Highway 1.

The Naval Gun Line

While the preeminent role of American air power in countering Hanoi's Easter Offensive has been widely reported and a is well-known aspect of the campaign, the important role—especially in the early days of the offensive—played by U.S. Navy surface combatants has often been obscured and underreported.

Bad weather and chaos on the ground greatly hindered air support in the opening days of the North Vietnamese assault against the 3d ARVN Division's positions south of the DMZ and intense enemy shelling effectively silenced most of the South Vietnamese artillery. Thus, the task of providing desperately needed fire support to the defenders fell to the handful of U.S. Navy destroyers steaming off the coast of Quang Tri Province. The USS *Joseph Strauss* and USS *Buchanan* began providing covering fire with their 5-inch guns to the string of fire support bases just south of the DMZ from the opening day. These ships were quickly joined by three other destroyers, playing a critical role in the South Vietnamese Marines' defense of the Dong Ha bridge and it was their accurate and timely shelling of attacking enemy infantry and tanks that helped stiffen the Mieu Giang–Cua Viet River defensive line in the early days of April.

Throughout May and into June the Navy rushed additional ships to the northern battlefield to provide increased all-weather defensive fire support in Military Region 1, as well as to assist in naval bombardment operations north of the DMZ against bridges, key road junctions, radar installations, anti-aircraft sites, and coastal defense batteries as far north as Vinh. At one point there were more than 40 ships on the naval gun line off Vietnam, including the cruiser USS *Newport News*, whose 8-inch guns could reach targets far to the west of Highway 1. Thanks to the presence of forward fire control teams attached to nearly every major I Corps unit, naval gunfire contributed significantly to the defense of Hue and the My Chanh River defensive line, as well as to isolated ARVN positions as far south as Quang Nai Province.

The deck of the USS *Newport* is littered with 8-inch shell casings following a bombardment mission against North Vietnamese targets. (Photo U.S. Navy)

During General Truong's northern counteroffensive beginning in late June, an average of two dozen ships were actively supporting the Marine Division's drive up the coast, firing an average of 4,000 rounds per day. Naval gunfire would not only be used extensively in support of the Marine assaults on Quang Tri city in August and September, but would prove equally instrumental in repelling repeated North Vietnamese efforts to dislodge the Marine forces blocking supply routes northeast of the city during the campaign. Over the course of the Easter Offensive ships of the Seventh Fleet would expend more than 16,000 tons of ordnance. As the fighting petered out by the end of October, the number of surface combatants was drastically scaled back as ships were released from combat duty. Nonetheless, a significant task force would remain on station and on call off the Vietnamese coast right up until the time of the January 1973 ceasefire.

Recapturing Quang Tri City

As July turned into August, the South Vietnamese fight to free the provincial capital of Quang Tri from the enemy's grasp remained stalled despite the massive aerial and artillery bombardment. Moreover, the battle had devolved into the grinding block-by-block fight that General Truong had sought so desperately to avoid, but political pressure from Saigon

ARVN troops counterattacking south of An Loc following the lifting of the siege in June 1972.

forced his hand. Now the apparent success of the entire counteroffensive was dependent on the recapture of Quang Tri, a task that would fall squarely on the shoulders of the Marines. It would be up to them to get the job done. Facing the Marine attackers would be the recently arrived 325C NVA Division and the surviving elements of the 308th and 320B NVA divisions—an enemy that appeared increasingly determined to fight to the last man.

Although the constant air strikes and artillery shelling had reduced much of Quang Tri to ruins over the past month, the city was laced with an extensive network of bunkers and tunnels and the old imperial citadel with its 30-inch-thick walls remained a defiant symbol of resistance, withstanding repeated South Vietnamese assaults. Despite having the city now encircled on three sides and troops from the 258th Marine Brigade pushing to within 200 yards of the citadel, they found themselves facing a deadly no-man's land and subject to heavy enemy artillery and mortar fire. Like the paratroopers before them, they too were unable to dislodge the communist defenders from the citadel.

The North Vietnamese were facing their own set of serious and growing problems too, admitting privately on August 9 that the South Vietnamese attacks had resulted in a "relatively rapid attrition" of their forces.[12] With the Marines blocking Route 560 to the northeast, supplies, ammunition, and reinforcements had to be ferried over the Thanh Han River, making them highly vulnerable to air attack. Units that had been fighting since March 30 were worn to the bone and their ranks severely ravaged with some NVA battalions having been reduced to a mere 50 or 60 men. Likewise, the constant shelling and air strikes shattered nerves and "the tempo of the bombing and shelling reached such a level that it was not possible to distinguish individual explosions," according to one official North Vietnamese account of the battle, and "one still suffered bleeding from one's nose, mouth" even when in a well-protected bunker.[13]

Nonetheless, there was still fight left in the enemy. During August, four NVA regiments hurled themselves repeatedly against the Marines of the 147th Brigade in

Brigadier General Le Van Hung (center) celebrates with President Thieu following the victory at An Loc, July 7, 1972.

Although the big B-52 bombers captured much of the headlines, F-4 Phantoms remained the mainstay of the Air Force bombing effort in both the North and the South. (Photo National Museum of the U.S. Air Force)

an attempt to reopen Route 560. They failed. Then on August 22, following a massive 3,000-round artillery and mortar bombardment, North Vietnamese infantry backed by a handful of tanks stormed across the no-man's land south of the citadel, crashing into the 258th Marine Brigade's positions. Following the initial shock, the Marines responded aggressively, pushing the enemy back after inflicting heavy casualties on the attackers.

Under growing pressure from Saigon for results and with Truong increasingly confident that a new effort stood a good chance of success given the now severely weakened state of the enemy,[14] Truong prepared for one final push in early September. First, he realigned his forces to free up the entire 147th Marine Brigade by having the Rangers move into the blocking position on Route 560 and moved elements of the Airborne Division into position to cover the Marine Division's left flank. Now General Lan would have two full brigades of his Marines for the final assault and be able to attack the city from multiple angles. Finally, as a diversionary measure on the day of the assault, he sent a U.S. Navy amphibious force with some 400 Rangers to the mouth of the Cua Viet River about ten miles northeast of Quang Tri to draw enemy troops and supporting artillery away from the front lines.

With the North Vietnamese still reeling from the preliminary bombardment and confused by the invasion feint behind their lines, General Lan gave the order to advance on September 9. The Marines of the 258th Brigade stormed across the killing zone south of the citadel, while the men of the 147th Brigade thrust from the northeast toward the center of the city. After several days of brutal combat, a battalion of the 258th Brigade battled its way into the citadel complex on September 11, where it was able to establish a foothold despite repeated enemy counterattacks. Meanwhile, a battalion of the 147th Brigade pushed its way through the north of the city to the Thanh Han River, while two other battalions from the brigade fought their way southwest through the streets to link up with their fellow Marines of the 258th Brigade on the morning of September 15.

After more than a week of heavy fighting that had left some 2,767 enemy dead,[15] on September 16 the citadel was secured and the South Vietnamese flag once again flew over the city. The final provincial capital was back in government hands.

The victory came at a high cost to the Marines, who suffered more than 5,000 casualties since the counteroffensive began in June, almost 25 percent of the entire Marine Division. Moreover, 3,658 of these casualties occurred during the seven-week battle for the city, which was an indication of the ferocity of the combat.[16] Praise was heaped on General Truong and President Thieu visited the front to personally congratulate General Lan and many individual Marines for their part in the victory. The most telling praise, however, came from the Marines' American adviser, Lieutenant Colonel Turley. According to Turley, the "Vietnamese marines, short in stature, rich in courage, and full of determination, stood tall in the eyes of all marines."[17]

Although fighting in the north, as well as across the rest of the country, would continue for the next several months, the recapture of Quang Tri city and the subsequent push northward toward the Cua Viet River signaled the end of the Easter Offensive. It also marked the failure of Hanoi's bid to turn the tide of battle on the southern battlefield and achieve a resounding military victory that would allow it to dictate the terms of peace. Peace, if it were to come at all, would now have to be achieved by the diplomats negotiating in Paris.

Throughout the summer, North Vietnamese commanders launched several unsuccessful attempts to slow General Truong's advance on Quang Tri city.

6. STALEMATE AMID PEACE TALKS

The recapture of Quang Tri city in mid-September would become the final visible signal of the failure of Hanoi's Nguyen Hue campaign and the beginning of the end of Saigon's counteroffensive. Even more telling after some six months of intense bloodletting and destruction that left both sides exhausted and staggering to the finish line, the strategic military balance in the South remained largely unaltered. Le Duan's gamble to turn the tables on the South Vietnamese and Americans on the battlefield had come to naught. True, the North Vietnamese now controlled more territory than before, but it was sparely populated and amounted to little more than "rubber trees and bricks" (jungle and a few small, heavily damaged towns), according to their own assessment.[1] Moreover, this "success" had come at a terribly high price in lives lost and equipment destroyed. It would take years to recover.

While having survived with its military intact, the Thieu government wasn't in much better shape and was incapable of exploiting Hanoi's weakened military condition, even as Washington rushed to make good Saigon's massive equipment losses. Most critically, the fighting had starkly exposed massive flaws within the South Vietnamese military, most notably its unhealthy dependence on American firepower to save the day. Saigon had come much closer to disaster than anyone wanted to acknowledge and the future of the country remained much in doubt once the Americans were gone. If there was to be any hope in bringing the war to an end now, it most likely would have to done by the diplomats in Paris and not by the soldiers on the battlefields of South Vietnam.

B-52 pilots and crew on Guam listen intently to pre-mission briefing, December 1972. (Photo U.S. Air Force)

Military Standoff

By October the fighting related to the Easter Offensive was largely over—although a new threat was emerging in IV Corps' area of responsibility in the Mekong Delta—and a military stalemate was in the offing as both sides tried to find their footing in the aftermath.

After three months of intensive fighting, General Truong's counteroffensive in the north had run its course and the military situation in MR 1 "was completely stabilized"[2] as the monsoon rains began. The Airborne Division had further secured Truong's western flank in Quang Tri Province after retaking fire support bases Barbara and Anne south of the Thach Han River. Activity in the Marine sector south of the Cua Viet River had fallen off markedly and in Quang Nam Province to the south the enemy had withdrawn back up the Que Son Valley, ending any threat to Highway 1 and Saigon's lines of communication. For their part, the North Vietnamese pulled back to their jungle sanctuaries to recover while still maintaining pressure on ARVN forces through periodic probes. Their most intense focus, however, was on rebuilding their battered logistics network to better supply NVA troops in the South. Roads and infiltration routes leading eastward from the Ho Chi Minh Trail through Laos were upgraded and the facilities at the captured river port of Dong Ha were expanded, so much so that within a year more than 20 percent of the war matériel destined for the front came across its docks.[3]

The same uneasy balance now prevailed in the Central Highlands. Several attempts in October to enlarge the government zone of control along Route 14 north of Vo Dinh made only minor progress. The North Vietnamese also remained well embedded to the north and east of Kontum, safeguarding their lines of communication into Laos and Cambodia and allowing traffic to move down the Ho Chi Minh Trail unimpeded. Kontum's Route 14 lifeline to Pleiku was open to road traffic, as was Pleiku's Route 19 to the coast and Saigon's forces were in firm control of the northern coastal plain of Binh Dinh Province and Highway 1.

Military activity in MR 3 around An Loc had largely come to a standstill in September with government forces content on securing the northern approaches to the city,

B-52s line up for takeoff from Andersen Air Force Base, Guam. (Photo U.S. Air Force)

but making no effort to take back Loc Ninh or the northern half of Binh Long Province from the North Vietnamese and an eerie silence descended over the ruined city.

While the three military regions that had seen the heaviest combat began to stabilize, fighting flared up across much of the Mekong Delta in the remaining months of the year. Early October saw two regiments of the 1st NVA Division move into An Giang Province and the Ha Tien coastal region west of the Mekong River, while other North Vietnamese troops infiltrated across the Cambodian border into Kien Phong Province where they clashed with ARVN and territorial militia forces. At about the same time, Viet Cong units south of the Bassac River moved to create blocking positions along IV Corps' lines of communication and infiltrate populated areas. This "clearly indicated an attempt by the enemy to extend his presence over the Delta, undoubtedly in preparation for a standstill cease-fire,"[4] but declined sharply when the ceasefire failed to materialize.

The enemy was back at it again in early November when elements of the 7th ARVN Division engaged regiments of the 1st and 5th NVA divisions attempting to infiltrate into northern Kien Phong and Kien Tuong provinces. During a series of engagements near the Cambodian border government troops inflicted heavy casualties on the enemy,

SA-2 surface-to-air missiles—with an effective range of 30 miles and able to reach altitudes of nearly 60,000 feet—posed the greatest threat to U.S. aircraft in 1972. All 15 B-52 bombers lost during Linebacker II would be to SA-2s. (Photo National Museum of the U.S. Air Force)

including the complete annihilation of a battalion of the 207th NVA Regiment that also resulted in the capture of 73 prisoners.[5] On the far western frontier Ranger forces were also successful in capturing large amounts of supplies and maiming two regiments, with one captured enemy officer admitting that his battalion had being so severely mauled by ground attacks and air strikes that it had only 30 men left.[6]

With the battle lines now largely frozen, both sides licking their wounds, and glad for the lull in fighting, attention turned toward peace talks in Paris in the fall of 1972 where Hanoi and Saigon would have to wait to see if the diplomats could produce a victory that soldiers in the field had failed to do.

Peace is in the Air

As early as mid-July, even with the ongoing fighting and General Truong's counteroffensive in the north in full swing, Washington and Hanoi had come to realization that diplomacy was "the best means for ending the war on the most favorable terms they could hope to achieve"[7] and the battle to determine South Vietnam's future now moved to the negotiating table in Paris. For Hanoi the confluence of the military failure of the Easter Offensive and the upcoming U.S. presidential election in November gave it a new sense of urgency. Failure to reach some kind of settlement before Nixon's reelection—which the North Vietnamese saw as all but certain by this time—might risk an even more extreme U.S. military response. Washington, for its part, had some leverage at the moment thanks to the vastly improved military situation in the South and the success of the Linebacker bombing campaign, but time was running out. The ongoing unilateral U.S withdrawal that saw troop levels falling to 27,000 by December 1 and the threat of a congressional cutoff of war funding meant this leverage could quickly evaporate.

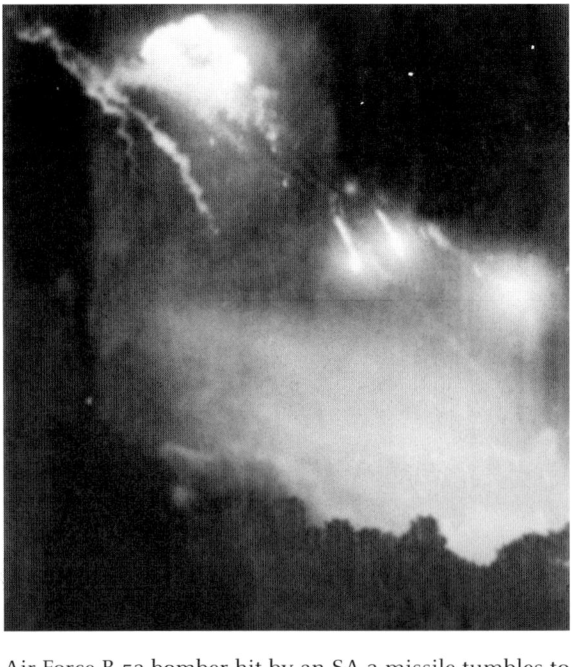

Air Force B-52 bomber hit by an SA-2 missile tumbles to the ground, December 1972.

Thus began an accelerated period of talks between the American and North Vietnamese delegations to break the three-year logjam and finally end the war. By early October the two sides had made significant progress to overcome, or at least paper over, their differences, although this increasingly came at the expense of South Vietnamese and the Viet Cong interests. On October 8, the North Vietnamese delegation handed Henry Kissinger a draft agreement of the minimum terms that Hanoi would accept to end the American military involvement and bring about a ceasefire. It was a turning point in the Paris talks. The North was now willing to make significant political concessions in the belief that ultimately it would triumph once the Americans were completely out of Vietnam, but Le Duc Tho insisted that the accord be signed by October 31.

The proposal, entitled "Agreement on Ending the War and Restoring Peace in Vietnam," called for an immediate ceasefire in place without waiting for all political issues to be resolved first; a total withdrawal of all American forces from South Vietnam, while implicitly allowing North Vietnamese troops to remain there; the return of all American POWs within 60 days; an implied, but murky commitment by Hanoi not to infiltrate more troops into the South; and the right of the United States to continue to aid the South Vietnamese and for North Vietnam to do the same for the Viet Cong. In addition, it call for the creation of an "Administration of National Concord" that would organize elections and make decisions by consensus, but not displace the authority of the Saigon government or Provisional Revolutionary Council (the Viet Cong), each of whom would run things in areas it currently controlled.[8] Most significantly, the North had abandoned its demand that President Thieu be removed and a coalition government installed in the South. It also omitted several other divisive and sensitive issues that could be addressed later, such as the presence of North Vietnamese troops in Cambodia and Laos.[9] As lead negotiator Kissinger was more than pleased at the North's change of heart and anticipated a major breakthrough.

The Paris talks now kicked into high gear and over the course of the next four days a tentative peace agreement was hammered out between Kissinger and Tho. The final product consisted of a 58-page draft for all four warring parties—the United States, North Vietnam, South Vietnam, and the Viet Cong—to sign. Despite the achievement, it was somewhat anti-climactic for Kissinger. "For nearly four years we longed for this day, yet when it arrived, it was less dramatic than we had ever imagined. Peace came in the guise of the droning voice of an elderly revolutionary wrapping the end of a decade of bloodshed into legalistic ambiguity," he later wrote.[10] Still, there were serious concerns among the U.S. delegation that the draft agreement would be a tough sell in Saigon. This would prove to be prophetic.

In the final stages of the negotiations Kissinger also requested that Nixon restrict the air campaign against the North as a sign of American goodwill. Nixon agreed and ordered a reduction in the sortie rate over the North Vietnamese heartland in mid-October and once the final details were agreed on, the White House ordered a complete halt to all Operation Linebacker bombing

President Nixon signaled his willingness to escalate the air war and break the peace negotiation impasse by sending B-52s against the North's heartland in December 1972. (Photo National Museum of the U.S. Air Force)

north of the 20th parallel on October 23. The five-and-half-month air campaign that had wreaked devastation on the North was over. It appears Nixon's forceful response to the Easter Offensive had indeed tipped the scales toward a negotiated settlement and the momentum for peace was so strong that Kissinger publicly declared on October 26 that "we believe peace is at hand."[11]

While Washington and Hanoi may have been ready to sign a peace agreement to end the war, the same could not be said for the Saigon government, which felt its vital national security interests had been pushed aside in the American rush to reach a settlement. This feeling of neglect and insecurity was further reinforced when President Thieu first learned about the terms of the draft peace agreement, not from the Americans, but from documents captured by South Vietnamese intelligence.[12] President Thieu and his closest advisers were incensed. They saw the proposed peace agreement as an utter betrayal of what they had just fought for by giving far too many concessions to Hanoi. It permitted North Vietnamese troops to remain in the South. It failed to create a secure DMZ that would prevent resupply and troop movements. And it allowed the inclusion of a national council of reconciliation that smacked of a coalition government. It was seen as "tantamount to surrender" and a death sentence on the Saigon government.[13]

To assuage Thieu's anger and overcome his feelings of distrust and abandonment the Nixon administration sought to coax the South Vietnamese toward acceptance. Kissinger pledged wording changes to the draft agreement to address their concerns and told Thieu that he had no reason to fear North Vietnamese forces remaining in the South, because Washington would "enforce the settlement" in the case of any massive violation.[14] Likewise, General Abrams gave his personal assurance by saying that President Nixon's commitment to South Vietnam was firm and that the military situation in the South was now secure. To back this pledge the White House moved to boost Saigon's military capabilities and provide it with a stockpile of equipment to defend itself after the American withdrawal. This golden handshake was to consist of nearly 300 fighter-bombers (including more than 100 advanced F-5s), the transfer of all existing A-1 aircraft in Southeast Asia to the VNAF, 227 UH-1 helicopters, 32 C-130s, 200 armored vehicles, equipment for three artillery battalions, and 2,000 trucks, as well as large quantities of spare parts, ammunition, and POL products.[15] Moreover, Nixon let it be known that future American aid was on the line if Thieu remained intransigent by saying that "were you to find the agreement to be unacceptable at this point" in light of concessions by the North, "it is my judgement that your decision would have the most serious effects upon my ability to continue to provide support for you and for the Government of South Vietnam."[16]

An F-4C Wild Weasel of the 67th TFS flies a Linebacker II support mission. (Photo National Museum of the U.S. Air Force)

Meanwhile, frustration at the delay was boiling over in Hanoi too. Le Duan and the politburo were growing increasingly annoyed with the Americans' inability to bring Saigon on board. Moreover, Moscow and Beijing were insisting that Hanoi sign and not jeopardize this opportunity to end the war. Seeking to shift the pressure back to Washington and Saigon, the North Vietnamese on October 25 released a chronology of the Paris talks, the key terms of the agreement, and the now-abandoned timetable for signing. Kissinger tried to put the best face on things and paint an optimistic picture, but he knew better. Amid Thieu's intransigence and Hanoi's re-hardening of its position, the best chance for peace in four years had just slipped through the American's hands. There would be no peace settlement. The war would continue.

A Return to the Battlefield

The failure to finalize a settlement in October cast a dark cloud over the Paris negotiations that not only undercut months of painstaking compromise, but seriously undermined any goodwill and the premise that all sides were fully committed to negotiating an end to the war. When the talks did resume on November 20, Kissinger's presentation of Thieu's lengthy list of 69 demands was met with a cold distain by Tho, who countered by presenting his own set of new demands. Moreover, Hanoi refused to discuss the withdrawal of North Vietnamese troops from the South, which was a non-negotiable demand

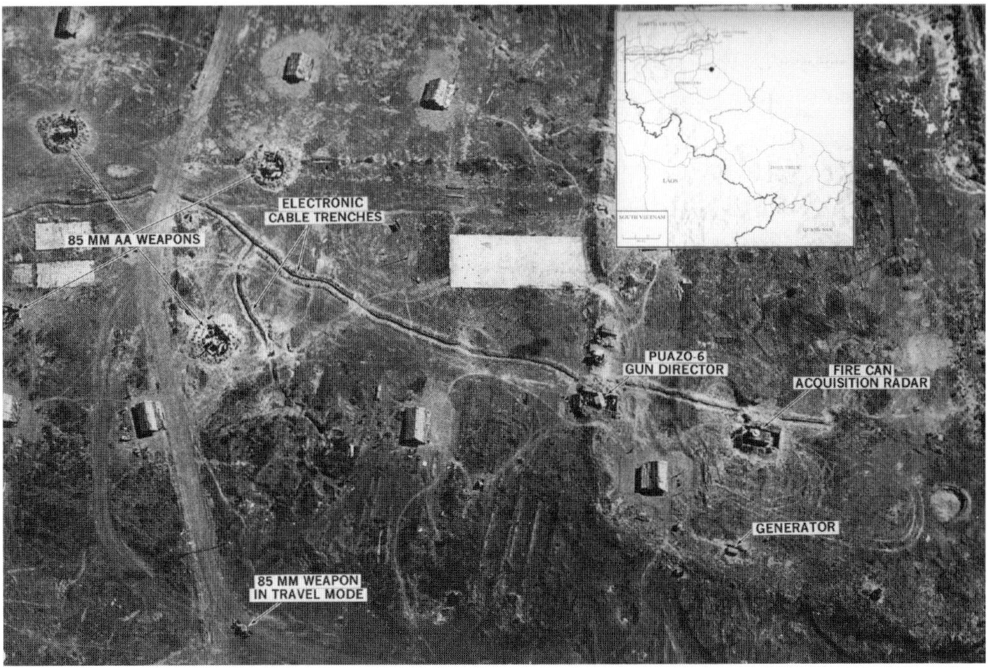

By late summer the North Vietnamese had established permanent air defense sites, like this 85-mm radar control position, in South Vietnam's Quang Tri Province. (Photo National Museum of the U.S. Air Force)

of the Thieu government. Things only got worse, the following sessions "degenerating into stonewalling, pounding fists, and issuing of threats," with the latter including a threat by Nixon to resume military activities if the North refused to negotiate seriously.[17] Complicating things further, Saigon launched an obstructionist public relations campaign in mid-December to derail the peace process, unless its concerns were fully addressed. With the talks stalled, Tho left for Hanoi on December 14 to consult with the North Vietnamese leadership on their next course of action.

Nixon and Kissinger were at the end of their rope. The American involvement in Vietnam was coming to an end and Washington needed to reach a peace agreement—one way or another. To incentivize Hanoi, while also reassuring Saigon, the White House moved once again toward using military muscle to break the deadlock. The deadline for finalizing a reasonable agreement was fast approaching. Hanoi and Saigon could be a helpful part of the process or face the consequences of an American-imposed version: the choice was theirs. On December 14 Nixon sent Hanoi an ultimatum to return to the talks within 72 hours or suffer the consequences. The day of reckoning was fast approaching.

For Saigon that day had already arrived. Although badly beaten and still suffering from its poor showing during the Easter Offensive, Hanoi still appeared intent on salvaging some battlefield success and improving its negotiating position by increasing its military activity in the Mekong Delta and attempting to cut Saigon's lines of communication in region. Thus, throughout November and into December the North Vietnamese made repeated attempts to infiltrate troops and matériel into the northern and western reaches of delta, as well as escalate local Viet Cong activity along Route 4 west of the Mekong River. Even more worrisome for Saigon were the long-term implications of Hanoi consolidating its territorial gains in the South to enable it launch a future offensive once it had rebuilt its forces. And the result might be vastly different next time. Thus, Thieu came to the realization that he no longer had any room to maneuver. He needed to placate Nixon, even if this meant biting the bullet on peace concessions, just as long as he could secure Washington's future security guarantee and the continued flow of military aid to his government.

With negotiations at an impasse and feeling backed into a corner at this point, Nixon decided to go ahead and unleash the most intense air campaign of the war. It was his last card to play and a huge risk, but if successful it would force Hanoi back to the negotiating table and end the war. "I don't want any more of this crap about the fact we couldn't hit this target or that one," Nixon told Chairman of the Joint Chiefs Admiral Thomas Moorer. "This is your chance to use military power to win this war."[18] The White House's weapon of choice would be the B-52 bomber, which for the first time since the one-off Freedom Porch Bravo raid against Haiphong in April 1972 would be used against the North's heartland. Its all-weather capability and tremendous payload made it the ideal airframe for the envisioned bombing campaign. But it was the overwhelming psychological impact of wave after wave of the big bombers dropping their deadly loads on Hanoi and Haiphong that was most appealing to Nixon. It sent an unmistakable message of American resolve to end the war.

At the time the decision was made to begin a new bombing campaign in December 1972, the Air Force could muster 206 B-52 bombers in-theater—54 B-52Ds at U-Tapao, and 99 B-52Gs and 53 B-52Ds at Andersen Air Force Base on Guam[19]—which was nearly half the Strategic Air Command's entire bomber inventory at the time. Though the B-52 force would be the centerpiece of the operation—codenamed Linebacker II—Air Force and Navy tactical strike aircraft, such as the state-of-the-art F-111, the all-weather A-6, and the advanced A-7 were also slated to play a major role. The plan called for B-52s to attack at night and then be followed by Air Force and Navy strikes during the day to maintain round-the-clock pressure. It would be a massive undertaking to execute and support with the American air order of battle ultimately topping 1,300 planes.[20]

From December 18-29 the Americans relentlessly hammered Hanoi and Haiphong both day and night as railyards, bridges, power plants, supply depots, and military installations felt the weight of the American bombs. The North Vietnamese tried their best to resist, inflicting significant losses on the B-52 fleet in the opening days of the campaign, but in the end, they were overwhelmed by American numbers and technology. Hanoi had had enough, agreeing to return to the peace talks in Paris.

It was the best outcome for all. Linebacker II underscored that Nixon was willing to inflict even more military, economic, and psychological pain on the North Vietnamese and since Hanoi was getting most of what it wanted, i.e., troops remaining in the South and control over territory it occupied there, it was not worth the risk of calling Washington's hand. Just as important, President Thieu got an unequivocal message of American military support and assurances of future treaty enforcement should Hanoi violate the ceasefire. This would prove to be enough to overcome the last remaining obstacles to peace. Within weeks of meeting in Paris in January 1973, Kissinger and Tho were able to finalize a peace agreement that all sides could claim as a victory. The fighting had come to an end, at least for now.

Even though the offensive had come to a close by early September, sporadic fighting continued for the next several months in the run up to a cease-fire. (Photo National Museum of the U.S. Air Force)

7. POST-MORTEM

Hanoi's 1972 Easter Offensive would go down in history as the greatest commitment of North Vietnamese regular forces and conventional firepower of the Vietnam War and one that came within a hair's breadth of succeeding were it not for the massive and unrelenting air intervention by the United States. Ultimately, Secretary General Le Duan's gamble to end the war by striking a crushing military blow against the Saigon government and forcing the Americans to acquiesce to the North's political demands failed in spectacular fashion. The North suffered up to 100,000 casualties, the loss of some 450 tanks, and hundreds of pieces of artillery on the southern battlefield (versus some 43,000 South Vietnamese casualties[1]), as well as having its country's air defenses shredded and its economic and military infrastructure crippled by American air power. The legacy of this failed military campaign, however, is so much more complex and the consequences more profound than anyone would have thought when the fighting finally came to an end in the fall of 1972.

North Vietnamese delegation at Paris prepares to sign the peace agreement ending American military involvement in the war, January 1973.

The North Vietnamese had always pursued a talk-and-fight strategy when it came to negotiating with the Americans, therefore the launching of a military campaign concurrently with ongoing peace talks was not without precedence. However, the timing of the offensive raised questions as to the wisdom of Hanoi attacking when it did, because U.S. forces were projected to fall to below 50,000 by July and then by half again by the end of the year. Why not simply wait out the Americans, who were on an inevitable path of unilateral withdrawal?

A combination of internal North Vietnamese party politics and largely unchallenged political and military presumptions appear to have convinced those in power of the need to attack in the spring of 1972—before the perceived window of opportunity closed. First, Le Duan, Le Duc Tho and their close allies had increasingly consolidated power within the communist party, government, and the military by mid-1971 by sidelining and marginalizing their opponents, notably General Vo Nguyen Giap. This gave them carte blanche—endorsed at the Twentieth Plenum in early 1972—"to accelerate the military struggle in the South" without effectively being challenged.[2] Second, there were growing concerns in the North Vietnamese capital that Washington's diplomatic efforts to woo the Soviets and Chinese were about to bear fruit, which could jeopardize future military aid to North Vietnam. Thus, Nixon's groundbreaking visit to Beijing in late February not only reinforced Hanoi's worst fears, but stoked the need for immediate action. Third, the North Vietnamese hoped to take advantage of anti-war sentiment in the United States and the upcoming presidential election to tie Nixon's hands and limit his ability to respond to any military escalation of the war. Finally, there was the widespread acceptance within North Vietnam that not only had Vietnamization failed, but that Hanoi's forces "had destroyed the backbone of the ARVN in Laos in 1971" and that military victory was within its grasp.[3] When taken all together, these factors were enough to convince the leadership that one final, strong thrust on the battlefield could end the war on its terms.

While the interaction of these factors helps explain the decision to launch the military campaign when it did, serious errors in judgment, misperceptions, and strategic miscalculations by the North Vietnamese leadership severely hamstrung the offensive even before it began and contributed to its ultimate failure.

In pushing for an accelerated struggle in the South that eschewed protracted guerrilla warfare and instead relied on the use of massed conventional forces, Le Duan and his allies played to the strength of the Americans and South Vietnamese. With Saigon's forces fighting a defensive ground battle, American air power (which was still considerable in early 1972) was the ideal tool for smashing Hanoi's infantry and armor assaults, hammering rear areas, and interdicting supply lines. Moreover, while the pre-offensive buildup of men and matériel was an impressive feat in the face of ongoing U.S. interdiction efforts in southern Laos, sustaining a 200,000-man mechanized force in the field was an entirely different matter. Thus, an exceedingly difficult logistics task became near impossible once American bombing and interdiction efforts in the North got rolling.

Likewise, Le Duan's desire to recreate a popular uprising in South Vietnam along the lines of the 1968 Tet Offensive was out of step with reality on the ground in 1972. The Viet Cong had never recovered from their beating during Tet and were in poor position to facilitate such an uprising. Meanwhile, the success of the CORDS program and government pacification efforts had undermined much of the communists' previous appeal at this point in the war. Despite this landscape, Le Duan continued to believe that some form of behind-the-lines popular uprising would be successful in tying down large numbers of Saigon's troops. Of course, the uprising never happened. Even in the old Viet Cong strongholds of the Mekong Delta region, the fighting there was but a minor sideshow during the critical months of the offensive.

Without a doubt however, it was Hanoi's grave misperception of Saigon's failed invasion of Laos during the Lam Son 719 campaign that led it to assume its forces "had dealt a decisive blow to Vietnamization" and this "easy victory blinded [party] leaders to the resistance they would encounter in South Vietnam in 1972."[4] Moreover, Le Duan and others viewed their 1971 success as the final nail in the coffin of Vietnamization. After all, NVA forces had gotten the best of Saigon's elite Airborne and Marine units and destroyed much of the invading armored force. But this was a serious misreading of the ill-fated campaign. The South Vietnamese had failed in an offensive operation deep into enemy territory that was plagued with leadership, command and control, and coordination problems. It would be a far different situation when Saigon's military was fighting a defensive war on its own territory with full American assistance.

While some ARVN units did indeed fold under the weight of communist attacks, the majority performed admirably—such as the 23d Division at Kontum and the 5th Division at An Loc—when push came to shove and South Vietnamese Airborne and Marine regiments proved to be instrumental in turning the tide of battle across much of the country.

Hanoi's most serious miscalculations, however, were political ones: it seriously underestimated the level of U.S. resolve and Nixon's willingness to engage in brinksmanship to secure an acceptable peace agreement and in how much the Soviet Union and China were willing to risk politically in the name of communist solidarity.

The American response to the invasion was not only "timely, forceful, and decisive,"[5] but Hanoi severely miscalculated Washington's ability to mobilize and employ air power on such a massive and destructive scale. It would cost Hanoi dearly. Although North Vietnamese leaders anticipated an American reaction and even prepared to weather another U.S. bombing campaign, they completely misread Nixon. Ending America's Vietnam involvement was important, but Nixon was not prepared to jeopardize the future credibility of the United States in the process by projecting weakness and abandoning an ally. "So realistically, we have to see it through, and the way is to stand by Thieu and support him," the president told his advisers.[6] And if this meant unleashing the full weight of American air power against the North Vietnamese, then so be it. Nothing was off limits, including an all-out bombing of the North's heartland or the mining of North Vietnamese ports and harbors. Critically, Nixon and Kissinger were even willing to risk antagonizing the Soviets and Chinese, because as they correctly assessed, neither Moscow nor Beijing was willing to sacrifice their global gains from improving relationship with the United States at the altar of communist solidarity. Thus, Hanoi quickly found itself alone, forced to face the full might of American military retaliation as its own resources were steadily depleted or destroyed.

As the tide turned on the southern battlefield by mid-summer and Operation Linebacker gained momentum in the North, Le Duan had little choice but to return to the negotiating table and privately admit that his gamble had failed. What little leverage he had gained early on was now gone and the Soviets and Chinese were now urging him to cut a deal with the Americans.[7] Reluctantly, Le Duan realized that getting the Americans out of the war would have to take priority. The liberation of the South would have to wait for now.

While Saigon's battlefield victory bought it time, it also exposed deep and serious flaws in its military and leadership that the Thieu government proved unwilling or incapable of correcting. The nature of fighting a defensive war across the breadth of the country against a determined enemy and without the ability to call upon a powerful ally to tip the scale in its favor would prove to be fatal in the end. Ho Chi Minh had been right all along: a grinding war of attrition and psychological warfare against your opponent's powerful allies was the model for success in South Vietnam, not an invading army sweeping to victory in a coup de grâce. It would take another two and half years to realize this goal, but ultimately the North would prevail in April 1975.

IT'S ALL OVER

Thieu Sends Thanks to America

PACIFIC STARS AND STRIPES

AN AUTHORIZED UNOFFICIAL PUBLICATION FOR THE U.S. ARMED FORCES OF THE PACIFIC COMMAND 10¢

Vol. 29, No. 28 Monday, Jan. 29, 1973

Peace Brings End to Draft 5 Mos. Early

WASHINGTON (AP)—Secretary of Defense Melvin R. Laird announced Saturday that "use of the draft has ended."

His action, placing the nation's armed forces on an all-volunteer footing for the first time in nearly 25 years, came five months ahead of President Nixon's goal.

In a message to senior defense officials, Laird said:

"With the signing of the peace agreement in Paris today, and after receiving a report from the secretary of the Army that he foresees no need for further inductions, I wish to inform you that the armed forces henceforth will depend exclusively on volunteer soldiers, sailors, airmen and marines."

Laird's decision cancels plans to draft about 5,000 men before next June 30, when legal authority to induct young men into the armed forces will expire.

Pentagon manpower officials said that the flow of volunteers, spurred by a series of military pay raises and improved fringe benefits, has encouraged them

(Continued on Back Page, Col. 3)

GI, Civilian Hikes Thawed

By MARC HUET
S&S Washington Bureau

WASHINGTON — The Defense Department Saturday announced the end of the military and civilian promotion freeze effective Feb. 1. The Pentagon also said the ban on hiring civilian employes is also lifted.

Deputy Defense Secretary Kenneth Rush, in a memo to the Army, Navy and Air Force, said hiring and promotions are authorized in line with President Nixon's 1974 budget.

"The austerity of the funding levels in that budget will require your continued attention to insure that only those personnel

(Continued on Back Page, Col. 2)

Secretary of State William P. Rogers signs the peace agreement in Paris to end the Vietnam war. The U.S. delegation includes (from left) William Sullivan, deputy secretary of state for Southeast Asian affairs; Ambassador William Porter; Assistant Secretary of State Marshall Green (partially hidden); and acting chief of the U.S. delegation at the talks, Hayward Isham. (AP)

Compiled From AP and UPI

SAIGON — The Vietnam war ended Sunday. It came to a halt at 8 a.m. as a cease-fire agreement went into effect.

Church bells rang out and the Saigon government voiced its gratitude to the Americans who helped it survive.

The cease-fire was underwritten

Related stories Pages 2, 3, 4, 6

a dozen hours earlier by the signing of peace agreements in Paris. A night of deadly fighting in various parts of South Vietnam preceded the hour of truce, however.

This last-minute effort to grab land left details of positions to be straightened out in the spotted pattern of disputed holdings that already mark the map of South Vietnam.

The four-nation group that is supposed to supervise the peace and pave the way for final agreements was in only preliminary stages of organization, and that too posed uncertainties.

It is, in fact, uncertain whether the 1,160 observers from Canada, Indonesia, Hungary and Poland will be effective even after the com-

(Continued on Back Page, Col. 1)

Groovin' With Mao

OMAHA (AP) — An Omaha teen-ager wrote Chinese Premier Chou En-lai that he thought China's national anthem was "groovy." Eighteen-year-old John Pirnot received a recording of the anthem from Peking — along with a bill for 40 cents. John says: "I was really surprised. I'm glad someone cared enough to help me."

Truce Hour Arrives, Attacks Raging

Compiled From AP, UPI, and S&S Vietnam Bureau

SAIGON — Although a cease-fire came to Vietnam at 8 a.m. Sunday, rocket and mortar attacks continued right up to the deadline, and explosions continued in Saigon even after the cease-fire.

An American was killed Saturday night in the last hours of hostilities, probably the last American to die in the war. He was the fourth American killed since the cease-fire agreement was announced Wednesday.

Explosions could be heard in downtown Saigon after the cease-fire went into effect. The U.S. command, flooded with calls, said it did not know the cause but recurring blasts sounded like an ammunition dump blowing up in the Saigon area.

Just before dawn, and less then two hours before the designated time of the start of the cease-fire, Communist forces slammed Soviet-built rockets into Saigon's Tan Son Nhut AB and adjoining areas. Military spokesmen said first reports indicated one Vietnamese civilian was killed and 15 were wounded.

At 7:55 a.m., U.S. spokesmen could say only that approximately seven rounds hit near

(Continued on Back Page, Col. 2)

Stars and Stripes headline of January 29, 1973 announcing an end to the war.

NOTES

1. A Gathering Storm

1. S. Lipsman and E. Doyle, *Fighting for Time*, p. 78.
2. Ibid., p. 76.
3. Ibid.
4. D. Schmitz, *Richard Nixon and the Vietnam War*, p. 82.
5. R. Nixon, *No More Vietnams*, p. 141.
6. E. Hartsook and S. Slade, *Air War Vietnam Plans and Operations*, p. 133.
7. M. Pribbenow, *Victory in Vietnam*, p. 262 and p. 274.
8. J. Morrocco, *Rain of Fire*, p. 100.
9. L. Nguyen, *Hanoi's War*, p. 228.
10. P. Asselin, *A Bitter Peace*, p. 38.
11. D. Fulghum and T. Maitland, *South Vietnam on Trial*, p. 122.
12. Ibid., p. 120.
13. Pribbenow, p. 285.
14. Ibid., p. 286.
15. Ibid.
16. Fulghum and Maitland, p. 122.

2. To the Sound of the Bugles

1. Nguyen Hue was the birth name of Emperor Quang Trung, one of the most successful Vietnamese military leaders, revered for his defeat of invading Chinese forces in the late 18th century. Both the North and South followed the convention of naming their military campaigns after historic Vietnamese figures during the war.
2. D. Andrade, *America's Last Vietnam Battle*, p. 51.
3. Q. Truong, *The Easter Offensive of 1972*, p. 16.
4. There are conflicting accounts surrounding the surrender. Despite suffering from heavy shelling for several days, the regiment's American adviser believed the position could hold out for "at least another week." However, a cabal of disaffected officers, including the anti-American" executive officer convinced Colonel Pham Van Dinh to surrender. Other more sympathetic accounts feel Dinh acted to prevent any further loss of life given his hopeless position and had little choice. See D. Fulghum and T. Maitland, *South Vietnam on Trial*, p. 140; Andrade, pp. 78-90; and Truong, pp. 29-30.
5. Truong, p. 30.
6. Andrade, p. 69.
7. Truong, p. 33.
8. G. Turley, *The Easter Offensive*, p. 241.
9. Quang Trung, was the imperial name of Nguyen Hue and was an allusion to the same historical events that the North Vietnamese were exploiting in naming their offensive after Nguyen Hue. Turley, p. 248.
10. Turley, p. 250.
11. Andrade, p. 333.
12. M. Pribbenow, *Victory in Vietnam*, p. 295.

13. Andrade, p. 373. For their part the South Vietnamese claimed to have killed 2,150 of the enemy during the battle of Loc Ninh, while acknowledging the loss of 3,000 of their own men killed or captured. L. Thi, *Hell in An Loc*, p. 62.
14. Two Americans (including Lieutenant Colonel Richard Schott, the regimental senior adviser) were killed in the battle, four were captured and released in January 1973 following the signing of the Paris peace accords, and one escaped and made his way back to An Loc. Andrade, note 16, p. 525.
15. C. Hobson, *Vietnam Air Losses*, pp. 222-223.
16. L. Thi, *Hell in An Loc*, p. 80.
17. Ibid., p. 81.
18. Fulghum and Maitland, p. 151.
19. Thi, p. 84.
20. Truong, p. 122.
21. Andrade, p. 393.
22. Ibid., p. 404.
23. Fulghum and Maitland, p. 154.
24. Pribbenow, p. 294.
25. Fulghum and Maitland, p. 156.
26. Andrade, p. 253.
27. W. Isaacson, *Kissinger*, p. 417.
28. J. Morrocco, *Rain of Fire*, p. 102.
29. E. Hartsook and S. Slade, *Air War Vietnam*, p. 221.
30. R. Francillon, *Tonkin Gulf Yacht Club*, pp. 126, 131, 135.
31. Morrocco, p. 109; Hartsook and Slade, pp. 290-291; D. Middleton, *Air War – Vietnam*, p. 125.
32. Morrocco, p. 108.
33. Fulghum and Maitland, p. 153.
34. Andrade, p. 266.
35. Hartsook and Slade, p. 284.
36. W. Thompson, *To Hanoi and Back*, p. 227.
37. W. Boyne, "Breaking the Dragon's Jaw," *Air Force Magazine*, p. 60; Thompson, p. 235.
38. Morrocco, p. 110.
39. Ibid.
40. Ibid., p. 131

3. Teetering on the Brink

1. G. Turley, *The Easter Offensive*, p. 290.
2. Turley, p. 290; W. Baker, "The Easter Offensive of 1972" cites the death toll at between 1,000 and 2,000.
3. D. Andrade, *America's Last Vietnam Battle*, p. 145.
4. Q. Truong, *The Easter Offensive of 1972*, p. 61.
5. D. Fulghum and T. Maitland, *South Vietnam on Trial*, p. 150.
6. Andrade, p. 147.
7. Ibid., p. 148.
8. Truong, p. 54.
9. Andrade, p. 161.
10. C. Hobson, *Vietnam Air Losses*, pp. 223-227.
11. Andrade, p. 170.
12. Ibid., p. 168.
13. Ibid., p. 167.

14. Ibid., p. 171.
15. Truong, p. 128.
16. Andrade, p. 430.
17. Truong, p. 130.
18. Andrade, p. 434.
19. Fulghum and Maitland, p. 154.
20. Andrade, p. 441.
21. Andrade, p. 455. Truong, p. 234, puts the casualty number at a more modest 10,000.
22. Andrade, p. 282.
23. Tube-launched, optically tracked, wire-guided (TOW) anti-tank rockets had just recently come into the U.S. military inventory and the Army was still experimenting with mounting them on helicopters at the time of the Easter Offensive. Three specially equipped UH-1Bs had arrived in the Pleiku in late April and would be rushed to the battle for Kontum by John Paul Vann. By the end of the offensive, TOWs would be credited with 47 kills—24 against tanks—against enemy vehicles, artillery, and gun emplacements. Andrade, p. 282.
24. Truong, p. 98.
25. Andrade, p. 299.
26. Ibid., p. 329.
27. Ibid., p. 325.
28. E. Hartsook and S. Slade, *Air War*, p. 312.

4. America's Aerial Counteroffensive

1. J. Smith, *The Linebacker Raids*, p. 73.
2. J. Ethell and A. Price, *One Day in a Long War*, pp. 50-51.
3. Ibid., p. 50.
4. C. Hobson, *Vietnam Air Losses*, p. 224.
5. W. Thompson, *To Hanoi and Back*, p. 35.
6. Ibid., p. 36.
7. Ethell and Price, p. 50.
8. Ibid., p. 131.
9. Smith, p. 73; Hobson pp. 224-225.
10. J. Morrocco, *Rain of Fire*, p. 136.
11. Ibid.
12. E. Hartsook and S. Slade, *Air War Vietnam Plans and Operations*, p. 298.
13. Hobson, pp. 224-227.
14. S. Emerson, *Air War Over North Vietnam*, p. 48.
15. Thompson, pp. 242-243.
16. Hobson, p. 220.
17. M. Michel, *The 11 Days of Christmas*, pp. 49-50, 89.
18. Thompson, p. 244; D. Middleton, *Air War – Vietnam*, p. 258.
19. Hobson, pp. 225-226.
20. Morrocco, p. 141.
21. Thompson, p. 237.
22. Eschmann, pp. 30-31.
23. Morrocco, p. 130.
24. Hartsook and Slade, p. 298.
25. Project CHECO Report, "Linebacker: Overview of the First 120 Days," p. 25.
26. Smith, p. 84.
27. Morrocco, p. 136.
28. Thompson, p. 248.

29. Ibid.
30. Hartsook and Slade, p. 299; Smith, p. 83.
31. Smith, p. 84; Morrocco, p. 138.
32. Morrocco, p. 136.
33. Hartsook and Slade, p. 301.
34. Ibid.
35. S. Emerson, *Vietnam's Final Air Campaign*, p. 71
36. Hobson, "Table: Fixed Wing Losses to MiGs," p. 271; Morrocco, p. 145.
37. Hobson, "Table: Fixed Wing Losses to Surface-to Air Missiles," pp. 270-271.
38. Morrocco, p. 140.
39. P. Asselin, *A Bitter Peace*, pp. 60-62.

5. Saigon Counterattacks

1. Q. Truong, *The Easter Offensive of 1972*, p. 65.
2. D. Andrade, *America's Last Vietnam Battle*, p. 187.
3. D. Fulghum and T. Maitland, *South Vietnam on Trial*, p. 178.
4. Andrade, pp. 187-188.
5. Fulghum and Maitland, p. 181.
6. Andrade, p. 181.
7. Ibid., p. 191.
8. C. Hobson, *Vietnam Air Losses*, p. 234.
9. As cited in Andrade, p. 451.
10. Truong, pp. 149-150.
11. Andrade, p. 327.
12. Ibid., p. 192.
13. Ibid., p. 191.
14. Truong, p. 70.
15. Ibid., 71.
16. Andrade, p. 196.
17. As cited in Andrade, p. 196.

6. Stalemate amid Peace Talks

1. D. Fulghum and T. Maitland, *South Vietnam on Trial*, p. 183.
2. Q. Truong, *The Easter Offensive of 1972*, p. 74.
3. Fulghum and Maitland, p. 183.
4. Truong, p. 153.
5. Ibid.
6. Ibid., 154.
7. P. Asselin, *A Bitter Peace*, p. 77.
8. W. Isaacson, *Kissinger*, pp. 447-448.
9. Asselin, p. 80.
10. Isaacson, p. 448
11. Asselin, p. 101.
12. L. Nguyen, *Hanoi's War*, p. 280.
13. Ibid., pp. 280-281.
14. Asselin, pp. 93-94.
15. Asselin, p. 92; E. Hartsook and S. Slade, *Air War Vietnam Plans and Operations*, p. 323.
16. Asselin, p. 95.
17. Nguyen, p. 291.

18. J. Morrocco, *Rain of Fire*, p. 146.
19. K. Eschmann, *Linebacker*, p. 77.
20. Eschmann, p. 77; R. Francillon, *Tonkin Gulf Yacht Club*, pp. 117-161.

7. Post-Mortem

1. D. Andrade, *America's Last Vietnam Battle*, p. 487. Although Andrade also notes that unofficial South Vietnamese casualties may have been more than twice as high.
2. L. Nguyen, *Hanoi's War*, p. 239.
3. Ibid., p. 243.
4. Ibid., p. 228.
5. Q. Truong, *The Easter Offensive of 1972*, p. 179.
6. D. Schmitz, *Richard Nixon and the Vietnam War*, p. 137.
7. Nguyen, p. 261.

BIBLIOGRAPHY

Andrade, Dale. *America's Last Vietnam Battle: Halting Hanoi's 1972 Easter Offensive*. Lawrence, KS: University Press of Kansas, 2001.

Asselin, Pierre. *A Bitter Peace: Washington, Hanoi, and the Making of the Paris Agreement*. Chapel Hill, NC: University of North Carolina Press, 2002.

Barker, W. "The Easter Offensive of 1972: A Failure to Use Intelligence," *Small Wars Journal*. Found at: https://smallwarsjournal.com/jrnl/art/the-easter-offensive-of-1972-a-failure-to-use-intelligence

__________. "The Easter Offensive of 1972: A Prelude to Vengeance Achieved, *Small Wars Journal*. Found at: https://smallwarsjournal.com/jrnl/art/easter-offensive-1972-prelude-vengeance-achieved

Boyne, Walter. "Breaking the Dragon's Jaw." *Air Force Magazine*, August 2011.

Emerson, Stephen. *Air War Over North Vietnam: Operation Rolling Thunder, 1965–1968*. Barnsley, UK: Pen & Sword Military, 2018.

__________. *Vietnam's Final Air Campaign: Operation Linebacker I & II, May–December 1972*. Barnsley, UK: Pen & Sword Military, 2019.

Eschmann, Karl. *Linebacker: The Untold Story of the Air Raids over North Vietnam*. New York: Ivy Books, 1989.

Ethell, Jeffery and Alfred Price. *One Day in a Long War: May 10, 1972, Air War, North Vietnam*. New York: Random House, 1989.

Francillon, Rene. *Tonkin Gulf Yacht Club: U.S. Carrier Operations off Vietnam*. London: Conway Maritime Press Ltd, 1988. Naval Institute Press edition, Annapolis, MD.

Fulghum, David and Terrence Maitland. *The Vietnam Experience: South Vietnam on Trial, Mid-1970 to 1972*. Boston: Boston Publishing Company, 1984.

Hartsook, Elizabeth and Stuart Slade. *Air War: Vietnam Plans and Operations, 1969–1975*. Newtown, CT: Defense Lion Publications, 2012.

Hobson, Chris. *Vietnam Air Losses. United States Air Force, Navy and Marine Corps Fixed-Wing Aircraft Losses in Southeast Asia 1961–1975*. Hinckley, UK: Midland Publishing, 2001.

Lavalle, A. (ed.). *Airpower and the 1972 Spring Invasion. USAF Southeast Asia Monograph Series, Volume II, Number 3*. Washington, DC: U.S. Government Printing Office, 1976.

Lipsman, Samuel and Edward Doyle. *The Vietnam Experience: Fighting for Time*. Boston: Boston Publishing Company, 1983.

Isaacson, Walter. *Kissinger: A Biography*. New York: Simon & Schuster, 1992.

Middleton, Drew. *Air War – Vietnam*. New York: Arno Press, 1978.

Morrocco, John. *The Vietnam Experience: Rain of Fire, Air War 1969–1973*. Boston: Boston Publishing Company, 1985.

Nguyen, Lien-Hang. *Hanoi's War: An International History of the War for Peace in Vietnam*. Chapel Hill, NC: University of North Carolina Press, 2012.

Nixon, Richard. *No More Vietnams*. New York: Arbor House, 1985.

Olsen, James. *In Country: The Illustrated Encyclopedia of the Vietnam War*. New York: Metro Books, 2008.

Pribbenow, Merle (translator). *Victory in Vietnam: The Official History of the People's Army of Vietnam, 1954–1975*. Lawrence, KS: University Press of Kansas, 2002.

Schmitz, David. *Richard Nixon and the Vietnam War*. Lanham, MD: Rowman & Littlefield, 2016.

Smith, John. *The Linebacker Raids: The Bombing of North Vietnam, 1972*. London: Arms & Armour Press, 1998.

Sorley, Lewis. *A Better War: The Unexamined Victories and Final Tragedy of America's Last Years in Vietnam*. New York: Harcourt Brace & Co., 1999.

Thompson, Wayne. *To Hanoi and Back: The U.S. Air Force and North Vietnam, 1966–1973*. Washington, DC: Smithsonian Institute Press, 2000.

Thi, Lam Quang. *Hell in An Loc: The 1972 Easter Invasion and the Battle that Saved South Viet Nam*. Denton, TX: University of North Texas Press, 2009.

Truong, Quang Ngo. *The Easter Offensive of 1972*. Washington, DC: U.S. Army Center of Military History, 1980. Available through University of Michigan Library reprints.

Turley, Gerald. *The Easter Offensive: The Last American Advisors, Vietnam 1972*. Annapolis, MD: Naval Institute Press Leatherneck Classics, 2010.

Index

Stephen Emerson was born in San Diego, California into a U.S. Navy family; his father was a career naval aviator and his mother a former Navy nurse. Steve and his siblings grew up on various Navy bases during the Vietnam War. His father served two combat tours as an attack pilot in Vietnam flying the A-4 Skyhawk as part of Operation Rolling Thunder while flying off the USS *Midway* in 1965 with VA-22 and later as commanding officer of VA-146 flying the A-7 Corsair II while embarked on the USS *Enterprise* in 1969. Steve holds a Ph.D. in International Relations/Comparative Politics from the University of Florida and currently resides in Orlando, Florida. His recent books, *Air War Over North Vietnam: Operation Rolling Thunder, 1965–1968*, *Vietnam's Final Air Campaign: Operation Linebacker I & II, May–December 1972*, and *The Battle for Laos: Vietnam's Proxy War, 1955–1975* examine the American role and use of air power in the region during the Cold War.

Also by Stephen Emerson